a garden of
fragrance

a garden of fragrance

SUZY BALES

ReganBooks
An Imprint of HarperCollins*Publishers*

A hardcover edition of this book was published by ReganBooks, an imprint of HarperCollins Publishers, in 2000.

A GARDEN OF FRAGRANCE. Copyright © 2000 by Suzy Bales. All rights reserved. Printed in the United States of America. No part of this book may be used or reproduced in any manner whatsoever without written permission except in the case of brief quotations embodied in critical articles and reviews. For information address HarperCollins Publishers Inc., 10 East 53rd Street, New York, NY 10022–5299.

HarperCollins books may be purchased for educational, business, or sales promotional use. For information, please write: Special Markets Department, HarperCollins Publishers Inc., 10 East 53rd Street, New York, NY 10022–5299.

First paperback edition published 2002.

Designed by Joel Avirom, Meghan Day Healey and Jason Snyder

The Library of Congress has cataloged the hardcover edition as follows:

Bales, Suzanne Frutig.
    A garden of fragrance / Suzy Bales.—1st ed.
       p. cm.
    Includes bibliographical references (p.).
    ISBN 0-06-039341-6
    1. Fragrant gardens. 2. Aromatic plants. I. Title.
SB454.3.F7 B36 2000
635.9'68–dc21
                                           99-058698
    ISBN 0-06-098910-6 (pbk.)

02 03 04 05 06 ❖ / RRD 10 9 8 7 6 5 4 3 2 1

To Carter
It is because of you

contents

acknowledgments

No book is ever written without the influence, help, and encouragement of others. I would like to thank my father for reading and making suggestions on the manuscript in the earliest stages. He was always quick to encourage and say a kind word even as he was wordsmithing. Gina Norgard, my assistant, organized the rest of my life to allow me time at the computer. Barbara Winkler, the executive editor of *Family Circle*, honed my thoughts on fragrant gardens in the many articles I wrote for the magazine; she also taught me how to be a better writer. I thank Charles Elliott, who edited and shaped the original manuscript. He saw things I didn't and believed in things I did.

Carter, my husband and best friend, has always been encouraging and a great supporter, believing that when the time was right, the right editor would believe in the book as he did and see it through to publication. Chris Pavone and Cassie Jones at ReganBooks shepherded the book through all the editing, design, printing, marketing, and publishing stages to bring it to market, and I am grateful.

Thanks go also to my friends among the garden experts who shared their knowledge and opinion about scent: Allan M. Armitage, Pierre Benerup, Conni Cross, Rich Dufresne, Joe Eck, J. Barry Ferguson, Alice Recknagel Ireys, Roy Klehm, Martha Kraska, Kathy Metz, Edwin Morris, Rayford Clayton Reddell, Marco Polo Stufano, Andre Viette, Katy Moss Warner, Wayne Winterrowd, and Sally Ferguson of the Netherlands Bulb Flower Information Center. And last, but certainly not least, thanks go to my agent, Helen Pratt.

IX

preface: get a whiff of this

THE FRAGRANCE OF FLOWERS offers a whole new world of pleasures. There is an intimate quality to a scented garden that beckons you in,
insists that you linger, and, at times, draws you down to its level to breathe
its enchanting perfumes. A seemingly insignificant thing such as a fragrant
flower miraculously influences our thoughts, moods, and imagination, ultimately affecting our behavior. Perhaps this is why medieval gardeners
believed the perfume of flowers was God's breath on earth.

    Flower fragrance has always had the power to cheer me up, change
my moods, and stir memories of other times and places. I notice this most
when I wake up grumpy and head for the garden to escape the petty problems of the day ahead. Crawling around on all fours, weeding or planting, I
am not actively seeking out a flower's perfume, yet as often as not a wonderful scent will find me. It taps me on the shoulder and subtly enters the quiet
corners of my imagination, inspiring me to search for its source. When I find
it, I often pluck the flower and place it in my buttonhole to carry the scent
with me. How else could I move on to another part of the garden? I am a
sorry sight: muddy knees, hair flung back and combed by dirty fingers, a fragrant flower just beneath my nose, and a smile on my face.

    Intuitively I have always known that flower fragrances are tied closer
to my heart than to the logic of my mind, yet I seldom admitted it, fearing I'd
be thought a little daffy and much too sentimental. But I had to cheer when

*"Smell is the sense
of the imagination."*
—JEAN-JACQUES ROUSSEAU

I discovered that scientists long ago established that women's noses are more sensitive than men's, and that in all humans our sense of smell is linked to the same area of the brain that controls mood and emotion. I was even more delighted when I learned that science now considers smell to be the most closely associated of all the senses to the part of the brain where memory is stored. This made me feel empowered and unstoppable in spreading the word about the value of scent.

Even before I had scientific proof of the power of flowers to cheer me up, I was instinctively drawn to their powers. When an unpleasant job awaits me, such as a long car ride or a journey into New York City on a day I'd rather spend in the garden, I always pick a fragrant flower to carry in my pocket or lay on the dashboard for my private pleasure. It invariably cheers and calms me. Usually I grab a few honeysuckle flowers, which I pass on the way out the front door. If it is lily season, that's the choice—one flower lasts out of water for three days, and the car carries the scent even longer. I'm hardly the first to have thought of this: the Adirondack Museum has an antique car with glass flower holders mounted on either side of the back seat. And, as is the way of all good things, they circle back: Volkswagen recently introduced a car with a flower vase on the dash.

Gardeners, of course, have always known that flowers make you feel better. John Gerard's *Herbal* of 1597 sets out the power of various flower and herb aromas in great detail. I used to think them laughably exaggerated, but now I'm not so sure. For example, the scent of basil, Gerard wrote, "taketh away melancholy and maketh a man merry and glad." He considered sweet marjoram to be a cure for those "given to over much sighing," and the fragrance of violets was supposed to stimulate the appetite.

Oddly, I've experienced some of these same sensations in the garden. Working among the herbs, I am often calmed by the blend of aromas—although at times I am keenly aware that I am hungry. Smelling rosemary evokes grilled lamb, while sage reminds me of a chicken roasting in the oven. Cilantro is synonymous with salsa and evokes dreams of Mexican food.

The effect of fragrances associated with food is easily understood. It is harder to analyze the moods and feelings evoked by fragrances unrelated to taste. Scientists may analyze patterns of behavior, but each of us has our own personal experiences. The garden writer Wayne Winterrowd has told me how "the flowering of my grandmother's night-blooming cereus, which, in my part of the world, always grew in a pot on the front porch, was watched for, and stayed up for when it finally bloomed. (Whenever I see one of those plants, I still feel sleepy.) But intense flower fragrances always do make me feel faintly drowsy, and I wonder whether some part of the reason for this is that they have a soporific effect, quieting other, more jittery aspects of the mind, almost 'doping' the smeller. You'd have to ask the aromatherapists that. I only know what I felt; and it returns to me whenever I experience a gardenia or magnolia."

Heavily scented flowers affect me in almost the opposite way. My memories of gardenias are not from the plants but from the corsages we wore to church on Easter Sunday and to dances and proms and other social occasions. I always felt invigorated, ready to kick up my heels. In any case, scented flowers almost always lift spirits; they are my drugs of choice.

introduction

IF YOU HAVE BEEN STOPPED in your tracks by a wonderful scent, or if upon entering a room the scent of flowers has made you smile, or if you love to be given a bouquet of flowers for a special occasion, chances are you're already on your way to becoming a devotee of fragrant flowers. Better yet, if you cannot pass a flower without burying your nose in it and you're frequently caught with pollen smeared on your nose (a hazard particularly associated with smelling lilies), you belong to the exclusive club of gardeners for whom scent is deeply important. I'm convinced pollen on the nose is a beauty mark of sorts.

I've always appreciated a gust of floral perfume, but I've seldom paused long enough to identify a scent or to understand where it was coming from and why. Nor until recent years did I purposefully plant for fragrance. Gardening for scent crept slowly into my consciousness over the last twenty years, gathering momentum, like a child on a sled, until now I never purchase a plant or design a garden without considering fragrance. It has become an integral part of how—and why—I garden. It takes no more effort than any other approach to gardening, and is infinitely rewarding.

scent and smell
Fragrance is more complex than it might appear at first sniff. Plants convey scent through the medium of essential oils. These essences of scent are not confined to the blossom or even its

> *"While years hurry on, The flower fared forth, though its fragrance still stays."*
>
> —AMY LOWELL

petals but may be diffused through all the tissues of the plant—petal, leaf, fruit, seed, stem, wood, gum, or root.

A number of attempts have been made to classify flower fragrances, with mixed success. Roy Genders, a British horticulturist, classified them in terms of the chemicals predominating in their essential oils in his book *Scented Flora of the World*. He recognized ten flower scents and four leaf aromas. (See Appendix, page 142, on the technical analysis of scents by chemicals.) Since essential oils are not pure, his classifications are not exact. Some flowers qualify for two different classifications. Moreover, human beings vary in their perceptions of smell—some of us smell one thing, and others another.

Roses demonstrate the complexity of the problem. A report in *The American Rose Journal* in 1962 recorded the perfumes of 170 different roses under different weather conditions in the famous Hershey Rose Garden in Hershey, Pennsylvania. The author, Neville F. Miller, found more than twenty-five elemental odors, and combinations of these elements were needed to describe the roses fragrances. The majority of hybrid tea roses fell into seven elemental odors and combinations of them—rose, nasturtium, tea, violets, apple, lemon, and clove.

The scented essential oils that create these odors should not be thought of as fatty substances like cooking oils, although they too don't mix with water, either sinking or swimming depending on their specific gravity. They are volatile—that is, they evaporate readily at ordinary temperatures, throwing their molecules into the surrounding atmosphere. High heat is not a prerequisite, although warmth is necessary for most of the molecules to become airborne. Because essential oils vary in their molecular weights, some evaporate more readily at lower temperatures than others. Because of their tendency to evaporate so easily, essential oils are sometimes called *volatile oils* or even *spirits*, as in "spirits of turpentine."

Only when the molecules are airborne can we perceive them with our sense of smell. If you visualize in your mind's eye scent molecules floating on the breeze, bouncing off one another and dispersing, it seems a miracle that our noses are able to pick them up at all. But it helps explain the inconstancy

of a fragrance—the way the scent of a flower can be piercing and intense one moment and only faintly noticeable the next. Wisps of perfume caught on the fly can be subtle and fleeting, teasing and taunting, where on a still day or indoors a penetrating scent can be gut-filling and intoxicating. When the scent molecules are concentrated in a close environment, they are of course most easily breathed into our noses.

But our noses are sadly underutilized, although less so recently because of the growing popularity of aromatherapy. Helen Keller poignantly named smell "the fallen angel" of the senses. Handicapped by her blindness, she developed a sense of smell so acute that she could perceive a coming rain (I find it hard to believe, but I know it's true). The average nose has more than six million receptor cells, capable of distinguishing ten thousand different smells.

In this century, smell has become the least used of our senses. It still plays a major role in our lives in detecting danger—anything from a forest fire to burning toast. Our noses warn us to beware of a lurking skunk, rotten food, or a dangerous gas. But the pleasures of the natural fragrance of flowers and the enjoyment they bring are all but forgotten. Artificial air fresheners, scented tissues, and chemically simulated perfumes bombard our nostrils. Too many of us are tuned out to the subtler, more delicate fragrance of flowers.

what's the sense in scent? Why a plant

or flower is scented is a question still answered by supposition. One possible explanation is that essential oils are not *essential* at all, but are instead the waste products of the plant squandered in the air. A more widely accepted theory is that flowers use scent to attract the insects needed for pollination. The aroma of scented leaves, on the other hand, may serve to repel insects that could damage the plant.

Evidence for the attraction theory is not hard to find. For instance, a scent may be strongest when the pollen is ripe. The early-blooming cowslip

plant names consist of two words, the genus and the species. The genus comes first and identifies the plant's family name. The species name that follows is an adjective describing the plant. The species name often describes the plant's fragrance. Here is a list of the most common species names and what they say about the plant.

amarus: bitter

anisatum: anise-scented

aromaticus: aromatic; fragrant

balsameus: balsamic; yielding a fragrant gum or resin

caryophyllaceus: with a clovelike fragrance

euodes: sweet-scented

fetidus: stinking

foetidus: bad-smelling

fragrans: especially sweet-scented

fragrantissimus: very fragrant

glycosmus: sweet-smelling

graveolens: heavily scented; strong smelling

hircinus: smelling like a goat

inodorus: scentless

moschatus: musky

odoratissimus: very fragrant

odoratus: fragrant, sweet-smelling

odorus: sweet-smelling

olidus: stinking

osmanthus: fragrant-flowered

piperita: resembling peppermint

primrose, *Primula veris*, is sweet-scented when it opens, but once the flower has been pollinated, the scent disappears, as if its siren's call is no longer required. But mysteries remain. Flowers that are self-pollinating, such as snapdragons, do not need insects for fertilization; they guard against intruders with the closed mouth of their flowers and are naturally scent-less. Why, then, does the trio of hybrid snapdrag-ons—'Super Jet', 'Vanguard', and 'Venus' bred in 1963—boast a sweet clove scent?

scent and the environment
The fragrance of a par-ticular plant can be affected by a number of factors—whether or not the wind is blowing, the number of blossoms, the amount of moisture in the air and soil, the temperature, the light, the time of day, and the soil's nutrients. All of these can be calculated, at least to some extent. Yet there must be more obscure influ-ences. There are fragrances that call out to me, yet as I approach, they withhold their scent, silently smirking, I suppose, at my expense. The honey sweetness of the European linden tree, *Tilia* x *europea*, has taunted me this way for years.

The number of fragrant flowers in bloom obviously has much to do with whether or not the scent calls out to you on the breeze, but I am always amazed to note that some of the smallest flowers are the most strongly perfumed. The tiny bells of lily-of-the-valley and a pinwheel of jasmine could find me anywhere. Standing a few feet from a garden in sum-

mer, you will notice the scent of a single lily and overlook that of a lonely rose blossom. For the rose's fragrance to reach a visitor, it takes a whole blooming bush. To scent the air on a mild winter day, a thousand snowdrops may be needed, while a mere handful works wonders indoors. As Floridians know, it is possible to smell an orchard of orange blossoms several miles away when the breeze is blowing in the right direction.

For some plants, the soil makes a difference in the strength (or lack) of the scent. A few years ago, while taking my children on a tour of San Francisco, I remember walking up a path on Alcatraz Island and smelling a pronounced honey scent. Blooming on the bank above the stone wall was Jupiter's beard, *Centranthus ruber*. (I like to think its obscure common name, kiss-me-quick, commemorates the kiss of fragrance planted on a surprised gardener.) I can't guess how it got here—Alcatraz has never been known for its gardeners—but it clearly thrived in the dry infertile soil it found there, growing more lush and fragrant than when planted in my rich garden loam and watered regularly.

Clues to a plant's preference are found in their origins. Like the Jupiter's beard, many fragrant flowers (herbs in particular) prefer a dry, lean soil to comfort them, as if they were still at home on the Mediterranean. Too rich a soil saps their natural oils and deprives them of their scent.

In shade or inside the house, away from the drying glare of the sun, fragrance lasts longer. Heat normally brings out the fragrance in flowers; conversely, cold weather suppresses it. In Neville F. Miller's test with roses (see page 135), only a few were consistently and noticeably fragrant during cold weather: their fragrance returned when the weather warmed up. This phenomenon is also true with other flowers: Wayne Winterrowd tells me that the chocolate cosmos has no scent during Vermont's colder summers. Yet abrupt changes in the weather can stimulate surprising alterations in the intensity of scent—both a summer shower and a light frost can bring on strong displays of fragrance.

At different times of the day and as the flowers age, different components of the essential oils evaporate at different rates, changing some scents. The climbing rose 'Lady Hillingdon' smells of tobacco, but only in the early

morning, while *Rosa nitida*'s perfume is lily-of-the-valley, in the evening alone. Most often the richest scent is present just as the flower opens. Since light is a stimulus for buds to open and petals to unfurl, on overcast days activity slows and fragrance can be slight. An extreme example of a flower's scent changing in the course of the day is the Asian orchid, *Dendrobium nobile*, which has gained notoriety worldwide because its scent changes from smelling of newly mown grass in the morning, to a honey pot at noon, to primroses in the evening.

In nature there are no hard-and-fast rules, only a few generalizations, and even these have many exceptions. The sweetest smelling flowers are often not much for looks, as though a lovely fragrance were consolation for a less-than-spectacular appearance. The lightly colored flowers such as the purples, pinks, and mauves are frequently scented; rarely are red, yellow, and blue flowers fragrant. Most of the strongly scented flowers are white with thicker petals, although most white roses are scentless.

scent in families

As breeders hybridize flowers— seeking a broader range of flower colors, double petals, and dwarf stems— they are more often than not losing the flower's fragrance. Fragrance is a recessive trait, and two deeply fragrant parents can, and often do, produce a scentless offspring. So our old stereotypical assumptions about scent and plant families are often off the mark. It is no longer true to assume that roses, lilacs, and lilies are fragrant while daylilies and hostas are not. The fact is that many roses, lilacs, and lilies being bred today are without fragrance. Chaste cultivars exist everywhere. And in many families not known for their fragrance—such as astilbes, begonias, daylilies, hostas, and hydrangeas—there are fragrant siblings: the 'Peach-Blossom' astilbe, 'Yellow-Sweetie' begonia, 'Lemon Cap' daylily, 'Royal Standard' hosta, and oakleaf hydrangea come easily to mind.

Thanks to Mother Nature's never-ending creativity and diversity, we cannot make flat statements about scent. Plants in the same genus do not

necessarily carry the same scent, or dispense it in the same way. The rose family flaunts dozens of diverse perfumes ranging from the much-loved damask scent to raspberry, tea, and licorice fragrances (see roses, page 34). Even within the same species there may be variations: for example, shrubs of the Chinese littleleaf lilac, *Syringa microphylla*, differ considerably in scent, depending on where they are found.

perceiving and describing scent

Like taste, fragrance is personal and subjective. Association, culture, and memory play strong roles in determining our aromatic likes and dislikes, and in how we perceive a scent. There is no way to separate these influences. What to me is an intoxicating fragrance could be obnoxious to someone else. When I describe a scent, I am voicing my opinion, and in a way offering a challenge. I do so to give you the chance to measure our descriptions against each other, to help you clarify what you smell and how it makes you feel. Luckily, there is no right or wrong.

When gardeners agree on a plant's scent, their decision may well turn up as an element in the plant's common name—pineapple sage, lemon verbena, and chocolate cosmos, for instance. These all happen to be scents agreeable to nearly everyone. But there are other plants with perfumes so controversial that they are either loved or hated (see page 93)—paperwhite daffodils are a prime example. And beyond the question of controversy, many plants possess a scent or scents too evasive, too ambiguous, or simply too indescribably forceful to be compared to commonly understood "benchmark" scents.

One basic problem is that the vocabulary for scent is inadequate. Perfumers have one language, gardeners another. Both at times rely on comparisons to other well-known scents, whimsical descriptions, and how a fragrance makes you feel. I'm afraid I shall have to do the same, and perhaps suffer some of the same failures.

As described by perfumers, fragrances are composed of three "notes," indicating the order in which the elements of a given scent are revealed to the

nose. Put in simple terms, the top note is the first to reach the nose when the bottle is opened. Then the middle note reveals itself. The bottom note is what holds the fragrance together. A perfumer refers to the strength, carry, and trail of a scent. It can take time—a half hour or more—for the scent of a perfume to reveal itself. The same is true for a good bottle of red wine, which is often opened and "allowed to breathe" before being consumed.

Flowers, too, need time to reveal the nuances in their scents. It does sometimes happen, of course, that the better you get to know them, the more character flaws come to the surface. The scents of many peonies change as you breathe deeply, leaving a rank aftertaste or after-smell, starting out delightfully enough but ending on an off-note. Once you know this, you will keep them at arm's length.

Some plants have scents so distinctive that they have become part of the vocabulary of fragrance. Carnation, gardenia, lily-of-the-valley, rose, and violet are often used to define the scent of a less common plant—Korean spice viburnum *(Viburnum carlesii)*, for example, is commonly described as smelling like carnations. There are gardenia-scented daffodils, rose-scented geraniums, and violet-scented dame's rocket *(Hesperis matronalis)*; Oregon grapeholly *(Mahonia japonica)* is lily-of-the-valley–scented. Flowers delight in mimicking each other.

The beautiful foliage of the scented geranium family lacks its own scent identity. Geraniums play floral charades, masquerading behind the borrowed perfume hidden in their leaves, and even have the gumption to use their borrowed scents in their common names—rose geranium, lemon geranium, and peppermint geranium are the best known scents and flavors.

As gardeners, we can use the floral theater and their mimics to our advantage. Yearning for lily-of-the-valley scent when it's out of season in winter? Plant an Oregon grapeholly. After the true lily-of-the-valley flowers fade in spring, the false Solomon's seal *(Smilacina racemosa)* carries the same scent, and later *Rosa pimpinellifolia* provides it. If gardenia is a favorite scent, plant the Cherokee rose *(Rosa laevigata)* and the Burkwood viburnum *(Viburnum x buckwoodii)* outdoors and grow Chilean jasmine *(Mandevilla*

laxa) and the African gardenia *(Mitriostigma axillare)* indoors. You'll get gardenia fragrance. Perhaps it is the scent of violet you covet: plant dame's rocket and the dwarf iris, *Iris reticulata*, in the spring, and grow the annual mignonette, *Rosa banksiae*, and the *Crinum* x *powellii* for a violet-scented summer. Isn't Mother Nature grand?

Flower scents are frequently described in terms of food. As we all know, there is a close association between food tastes and smells and flower fragrances. Without a sense of smell, taste is boring indeed: the taste buds on your tongue distinguish only the four flavors of salty, bitter, sour, and sweet. It is the aroma of food that gives it its flavor. Without it, apples would be indistinguishable from potatoes, and carrots from parsnips. If you don't believe me, put a clothespin on your nose, shut your eyes, and have a trusted friend feed you bite-sized pieces of similarly textured apples and potatoes. You won't know which is which.

Such basic flavors as chocolate, vanilla, lemon, and mint are easily identified by almost everyone. Sniff a chocolate cosmos *(Cosmos atrosanguineus)* and you will quickly recognize the chocolate smell, while the vanilla scent of heliotrope is unmistakable. Carriers of lemon fragrance abound in the floral world, and some have the audacity to announce their theft in their common names: lemon balm, lemon thyme, and lemon basil, to name a few. The mints take another approach. There is apple mint *(Mentha suaveolens)*, peppermint *(M.* x *piperita)*, spearmint *(M. spicata)*, gingermint *(M.* x *gracilis)*, and so on. The scent of some flowers makes my mouth water.

Plant names involving the odors of fruit are quite common. They include the plum-scented grape hyacinth and the strawberry-scented bouncing bet *(Saponaria officinalis* 'Rubra Plena'). Pineapple is a popular scent borrowed most notably in the strongly scented pineapple sage *(Salvia elegans)*, and, of course, broom has copied it too.

Whimsical comparisons and flowery descriptions are used by gardeners as well as poets. So far as I am concerned, "Grandma's carrot cake" is the hands-down favorite for describing a spicy-scented dianthus. "Wine after dark" refers to the night-scented golden trumpet vine, *Allamanda cathar-*

tica, and "a chocolate peppermint patty" aptly describes the chocolate mint, *Mentha piperita* cv. chocolate.

I have heard descriptions that enlarge the imagination. Although I have never been close enough to a wet fox to smell its fur, it is easily imagined when smelling a crown imperial fritillary. But describing the fragrance of a flower is at best difficult. When I'm completely tongue-tied I may resort to saying how the smell makes me feel—delighted, intoxicated, revolted. In doing so, I am following a practice started centuries ago: In Elizabethan times lavender was described as a "comfortable" smell; a lavender-scented shirt made the wearer comfortable, even as it disguised body odor.

your fragrant garden It's my sincere hope that this book inspires you to make a fragrant garden, or at least to grow more fragrant plants. Nothing has to be sacrificed in doing so. The variety of scented plants available allows for fragrance in every color, size, and style imaginable. It might take a little more effort to locate a fragrant variety of a favorite plant, but it is surprising how many exist. Remember that it isn't necessary for every plant in a garden to be perfumed. The key is to have a number of heavily fragrant flowers in bloom throughout each season.

The more I have learned about scent in the garden, the more complicated, mysterious, and elusive it has become. Perhaps that is why I go on experimenting. With so many fragrant plants available, a lifetime is too short to get to know them all. Moreover, since many fragrances reveal themselves slowly, gardeners have to be understanding and patient with the plants they grow. Don't give up on a flower after one whiff on the grounds that it is only slightly scented or scentless; you might miss a lot. The problem could be no more than a strong breeze or too few blossoms to make their presence known, the heat of the sun, the lack of moisture in the soil, a chill in the air. Just as I would hate to be judged after a single meeting, flowers need time to reveal themselves to the gardener. Patience is a virtue and a gardener's greatest friend. Once one begins to follow one's nose, all kinds of mysteries and miracles can be sniffed out.

a garden of fragrance

1 planning and planting

MY OWN LOVE OF FRAGRANT FLOWERS started at birth. I'm positive that my father brought my mother a gardenia for her bedside when he came to see me for the first time. Certainly gardenias arrived at every important event and celebration throughout my childhood. Still, my devotion to growing fragrant flowers in my own garden started only a dozen years ago, recently enough for me to remember—and regret—my mistakes. I hope you'll learn from them; it could save you time and trouble. What I know is rooted in the context of my garden.

Since plants grow differently in different gardens under different conditions, I must first tell you about my own. It is on an island off the North Shore of Long Island. My husband and I purchased the house and six acres of land from the son of the last man to live there, more than twenty years ago. The carriage house was built in 1906 and the main house followed in 1908. When we arrived, both houses were in a tumbledown condition, sadly in need of renovation, and there wasn't a garden anywhere. The grounds were mostly given over to an unkempt lawn. A little more than one acre had been allowed to run wild, becoming a self-planted woodland of brambles, poison ivy, English ivy, and—mainly—tulip trees. The soil in this woodland area is still the best we have—loamy topsoil built layer on layer by the decomposition of

"Without charm there can be no fine literature, as there can be no perfect flower without fragrance."
—STÉPHANE MALLARMÉ

3

fallen leaves. A curving path leads through the woods to the beach, wide enough to accommodate a fire truck if need be. My first step toward creating a garden took place here. I started at the entrance to the woods and gradually worked my way to the water, taming the wilderness along the way by removing undesirable growths and adding favorite woodland plants I had loved at my previous home.

A large circle of impressive oaks surrounds the front lawn. They had been brought in, fully grown, by horse and wagon in 1908. Several wonderfully fragrant, honey-scented hundred-year-old European lindens *(Tilia x europea)* also grow along the driveway. Apart from these trees, however, there was not much contributing to a garden, fragrant or otherwise—patches of the wild rose, *Rosa multiflora*, a lonely *Rosa eglanteria*, a clump of 'Festiva Maxima' peony, a dozen Japanese iris, and a near-wild honeysuckle climbing the entrance to the house. Tilled ground where a vegetable and cutting-flower garden had once grown lay behind a chicken-wire fence.

Rumors persist that in the nineteenth century our land was occupied by a brickyard, and I believe it. Most of the soil is very heavy clay. While rich in nutrients, clay holds too much water, and I have drowned many a plant. This problem might explain the previous owner's failure to create flower gardens. I have to sympathize—the soil is the most difficult gardening problem I face. Raised beds have solved the drainage problem in the vegetable, flower-cutting, and herb gardens, while trees and shrubs on the front lawn and in the orchard have been planted on mounds of soil for the same reason.

We removed three apple trees leaning on their last legs near the porch at one end of the house, replacing them with a formal flower and rose garden. We enclosed the area with stucco walls to protect it from gales off the sea. It was necessary to build up the soil several feet at one end to make it level, and since we did this by trucking in and layering compost, cow manure, and topsoil in the beds, we were surprised to find that drainage was still a problem. But it certainly was—after planting five hundred perennials and watching them slowly regress over four weeks, I had to hire a gardener to help me transplant them to a holding bed while we laid elaborate systems of drainage pipes under the beds. Many of those first perennials didn't survive. It was a lesson hard learned.

Flower gardens around the swimming pool were easier to plant, because clay had been removed during the pool's construction and replaced with bank run, gravel, compost, and topsoil.

But it was the rock garden planted at the edge of the woods that taught me how far I needed to go before the drainage was really adequate. When the flowers spilled over the rock wall and seeded themselves willy-nilly into a place they preferred—the gravel driveway—I was forced to take it as a message from above. Acting on the flowers' suggestions, I turned the drive into a proper flower border (see Chapter 5). The soil there is light and sandy and the drainage excellent.

And so it was with me twenty-two years ago when we began work on our garden, fragrance was hardly at the forefront of my mind. I was so caught up in the miracle of growth that anything prepared to grow easily, even invasive plants, were welcome. Then I planned for color, since color makes an immediate impact. Next, having flowers through the seasons became important to me. And as the garden and I matured together, I began to care more and more about the subtleties of textures and foliage.

The tradition of segregating plants, each kind growing only with its own, was strongly entrenched in my thinking. First I planted an herb garden, then a perennial garden. A rose garden followed shortly after.

Since then my approach has changed radically. Now I say anything goes. Fragrant plants, no matter how they have been classed by the botanists, belong in every garden. Scented annuals play a starring role in the perennial garden, holding my attention for many months. My larger flower borders are anchored with scented shrubs or perfumed roses. I've learned that vines can anchor too. A rambling rose, honeysuckle, or fragrant clematis planted on a fence at the back of a garden spreads its arms to hold the garden together. Sweet peas and other shorter climbers may splendidly festoon a trellis in the middle of the flower garden.

Planning and Planting

A ruffle of herbs as an edging, parsley perhaps, can prove useful as well as decorative. Other herbs, catmint and lavender, creep in under the roses, where they discourage insects, keep down the weeds, act as a living mulch, and add much more color and fragrance to the garden. Roses, conversely, creep into the herb garden.

Today, bulbs too pop up in the strangest places. Top-heavy balls of sweet-scented alliums intermingle with the onion-scented chives in the herb garden, daffodils perfume the pachysandra, and lilies spritz their sweet breath from between the canes of summer-weary shrub roses or beneath the branches of vitex just breaking into bloom. I no longer pay much attention to the rules, and I like it like that. The beauty, the fragrance, and the manners of different plants decide where they are placed. This freedom allows me to pack in more scent per square inch than I might otherwise. Now my slogan is: Ponder, then dare.

Everyone knows it makes good sense to plan before planting; it's something I learned the hard way. But I also know, from having helped the landscape architect Alice Recknagel Ireys install many gardens over the years, that gardens never end up being planted as they are planned on paper. Two things happen. First, new combinations come to mind as the plants are moved around and set in their places. (I always stop work to take a careful look before they are planted.) Second, there are always a few plants that turn out to be unavailable at planting time, and rather than leave an empty space, something else is substituted. Nevertheless, in spite of the inevitable last-minute changes, concentrated time taken to plan the garden will open up new possibilities, and the result will be a better garden.

This is not a primer on garden design—plenty of those are in print—so I won't attempt to cover the basics of that art. Instead, I'll pass along my personal observations on how to pack more perfume into existing gardens and where to add plants for the most fragrant benefits. Remember that the best gardens are never finished, but evolve over time. A case in point is our lilac and peony walk, which evolved over a dozen years into a fragrant path (see page 22).

where to plant

Fill the areas in which you spend the most time with scented plants. You needn't worry about planting too many of them together. I've never heard a report of a battle of fragrance in any garden I've visited.

Consider your family's lifestyle. Do you entertain in your garden or on a terrace? Do you eat summer meals outdoors? A fragrant plant will be noticed more if it is located where you customarily sit. On the other hand, if you have a fragrant garden with no fixed sitting spot, place a chair or a bench so as to take advantage of the perfume and to encourage visitors to linger. Night-scented flowers should be grown around a porch or terrace where you sit outside at night, near an entrance or in pots to be conveniently moved about (more about this in Chapter 4).

A simple way to start introducing more scent into your garden is to replace unhappy or dying plants with fragrant ones. Beef up your borders with fresh scented plants or fill containers and group them near chairs and tables.

Which door of your house do you use the most during summer? Do you take a different route in winter? Choose the right spot and fragrant plants will call out a greeting each time you pass.

Consider the flower's season of bloom when deciding where to place it. With winter-blooming flowers especially, it is important that they be planted where we come and go regularly, as we so seldom linger in the garden in cold weather. Since many of these bloom before leafing out, plant them against an evergreen background that shows their flowers at their best in winter. Plant Chinese witch-hazel, *Hamamelis mollis*, and winter honeysuckle, *Lonicera fragrantissima*, so as not to miss their beauty when seen from indoors or miss their scent as you leave or enter the house. If you notice them blooming every day, it is easy to remember to bring branches indoors where the warmth will cause their rich scent to emerge.

Fragrance will be stronger if a garden is sheltered from the wind and designed to hold heat and moisture. While a garden protected on all four sides is ideal, it isn't always possible or practical. A semicircle hedge of holly protects our rose garden and helps stay the wind from across the bay. We chose holly because it is evergreen, but a deciduous hedge of lilac or mock orange would break the wind in summer and scent the spring air before the roses bloom. A house, a garage, a small island of fragrant trees and shrubs, a rose hedge, a picket fence festooned with scented vines—anything that blocks and slows the wind is helpful in capturing and bottling the perfume.

When deciding where to plant fragrant shrubs, don't confine yourself to traditional plantings. Tweaking tradition is the sport of every good gardener. A hedge of flowering shrubs, summersweet clethra, lilacs, mock orange, or roses is the friendliest way to mark a boundary or divide space to create garden rooms. The more fragrant shrubs in the row, the stronger the scent will be.

The areas next to a sidewalk, curb, or along the walk to the front door are seldom planted in suburban America, but they are a wonderful and often sunny place for a flowering hedge. Try an island planting, a simple oval or circle of shrubs, perhaps with a flowering tree such as the Japanese stewartia and its sweet summer scent in the middle. An island can divide a backyard, screen out an eyesore, stop the wind, and add a vertical dimension to make the space appear larger.

Evergreen foundation plantings might include the seldom-planted Oregon grapeholly *(Mahonia japonica)* and scented cultivars of rhododendron and azalea. Deciduous scented shrubs such as buddleia, daphne, viburnum, and vitex can be planted in front of existing evergreens, enlivening boring foundation planting with color and scent. You'll then have the best of both worlds—an evergreen skirt around the house in winter, and fragrant flowers in spring, summer, and fall. It also pleases me that enlarging the border means less grass to mow.

I love the European approach to small spaces. In Holland, flower gardens replace lawns in the front of town houses. The English, in their demand for privacy, put hedges everywhere—and plant more gardens inside them. We would do well to follow these examples.

A Garden of Fragrance

pack in more bulbs

A decade ago, probably out of a desire for richness of mature spring plantings (and, I admit, a general laziness), I started layering bulbs at different depths in the same hole. The result has been wonderful—a lush garden boasting a fascinating blend of bloom and far more scent and beauty to each square foot than before. The practice also makes it easier to plant a large number of bulbs with a minimum of digging.

Depending on your choice of bulbs for layering, the plants can all bloom at once or extend the season by blooming successively. At my house, daffodils bloom in a sea of blue starflowers *(Ipheion uniflorum)* and blue puschkinia after the snowdrops depart. The daffodils are planted nine inches deep, the starflowers five inches deep, and snowdrops three inches deep. The lower bulbs have no trouble growing up, around, and through the upper bulbs. Mother Nature has taught all her children to grow together.

Taking the design one step further, layer bulbs between a triangle of hosta 'Royal Standard' or 'Peach Blossom' astilbe. The latter sprout as the bulbs finish blooming, thus hiding decaying foliage and adding scent to the summer garden. Or layer spring bulbs in trenches surrounding spring-blooming shrubs such as tree peony, kerria, and forsythia. If the bulb's blooming time is the same as that of the shrubs, even better.

If you have existing patches of unscented ground covers, layer bulbs into them. Most ground covers, grass included, are great companions for bulbs. They protect the bulbs from freezing weather, keep mud from spattering on the flowers, and provide a green backdrop to spotlight the flowers' colors. Lungwort, ajuga, pachysandra, liriope, creeping euonymus, foamflower, and myrtle underplanted with fragrant bulbs bring beauty and scent to a scentless planting. Daffodils, wood hyacinth, snow crocus, snowdrops, and species tulips all naturalize nicely under ground covers. However, you must take care to choose bulbs whose flowers will be taller than the ground cover.

designing with annuals and perennials

Replacing wood chips or mulch with scented ground covers immediately improves the look and smell of a garden. Look around the hem of the skirts of existing trees and shrubs for places to cluster and mass bigroot geranium *(Geranium macrorrhizum)*, lily-of-the-valley, St. John's-wort, and sweet violets to create a perfumed pocket. Hay-scented sweet alyssum, clove pinks, sweet spicy peonies, and lemon-scented daylilies are good flounces around a sunny shrub.

I'm always a little hesitant about robbing the beauty of a flower border for bouquets for the house. (Not that it stops me; I can rationalize anything.) But a fragrant cutting garden is a better answer, furnishing flowers without guilt. It also makes it easier to share the pleasure that flowers give when taking a bouquet to friends or neighbors. I edge my vegetable garden with fragrant annuals and sneak early-blooming flowers between late-maturing vegetables. In spring, sweet peas climb on trellises that will be occupied by cucumbers in late summer. The vegetable garden is more attractive, and my craving for extra flowers is temporarily satisfied.

designing with vines and climbing roses

If I dwell on vines, it is for good reason: They are misunderstood and overlooked in many gardens. Even books devoted to vines are few and far between. Garden writers can't find enough to say about them, and often group them with ground covers. Yet vines clamber above us, and powerful perfumes drifting down from on high are especially noticeable and can carry great distances. Scented vines draw the eye upward, grabbing a little of the sky, bringing it closer to earth. After all, a touch of heaven is what a garden is all about.

Even when not in flower, vines tie the entire garden together with the lushness of the green background they provide. From a distance, the upward

reach of wisteria, sweet autumn clematis, and climbing roses directs attention to the beauty of all the blossoms: the less fussy the pruning, the higher the vines, and the greater the impact. Your eye keeps going to them. They add a touch of extravagance, while the vines themselves festoon and beautify what they cover.

Whenever I see bare arbors or gazebos I find myself dressing them in my imagination. A gazebo canopied with roses creates a fragrant bower, a suitable place for the heroine of a Jane Austen novel to sit and gossip—perhaps have a clandestine meeting. Today, a gazebo furnished with a table and chairs becomes a romantic spot for a leisurely meal, an afternoon tea, or a cozy chat.

Having covered both our gazebos with perfumed roses, I admit I got a little carried away when I set out to clothe the grape arbor. I had no worries about hurting our harvest; the eighty-year-old vines are so productive that we have always had a glut of grapes. So without hesitation I covered the bare, gnarled legs and protruding bony knees of the vines with colorful stockings of sweet peas and honeysuckle. At the shady end, leading into the secret garden, I planted three spring-blooming vines—clematis *(Clematis montana rubens)*, for its vanilla scent, wisteria 'Alba' for its penetrating sweetness, and akebia to add a spicy vanilla twist. Assorted roses were added to scent the summer breezes and sweet autumn clematis *(Clematis terniflora)* for a vanilla-scented fall. The grapes have hardly seemed to notice—but the rest of us certainly did.

Remember that if you have an existing garden gate, an arbor can be added in front or behind it. A glimpse through an arch garlanded with scented vines focuses the view and frames the vista as it issues a fragrant welcome and an invitation to enter the pathway. A perfumed path is always interesting and mysterious.

Don't ignore traditional places to grow vines. I have them climbing up a lamppost, on a porch pillar, and on the mailbox post. And I am not above using fast growers such as the two vanilla-scented, small-flowered clematis, *Clematis montana* and the sweet autumn clematis, to camouflage an unsightly building or a wall needing paint or repair.

We have recently lost a number of large trees to high winds. It is difficult and expensive to have the stumps removed. So I have taken to cutting stumps into solid chairs facing the best view and letting sweet autumn clematis slipcover them. When the clematis is in bloom, its sweet vanilla perfume scents the surroundings. Over time the stumps rot and disappear, just as I want them to.

Garages are usually more functional than beautiful. But they too can be dressed up by having an eyebrow of honeysuckle, clematis, or wisteria grown over the doors. The brow draws attention to itself and away from the oversized doors. At the same time it fragrantly welcomes your return. A tool shed planted with fragrant vines gives the illusion of a quaint country cottage.

My philosophy, as should be obvious by now, is to grow scented vines everywhere and anywhere—on fences, over walls, up established vines, through existing shrubs, and into trees. Adding a fragrant vine or two or three, you'll find your garden never was so lush, looked so beautiful, or smelled so sweet. Although it is often said that "for the most pleasing effect in a garden use restraint," I'll never accept it. With vines, as with flowers, more is always better.

movable scent Pots and tubs of fragrant flowers can be placed near outdoor seating areas, on each side of steps leading to the door and clustered on a terrace, or on any other hard surface to mimic a garden. The smaller containers can be carried into the house before the fall frost to extend the bloom indoors.

The procedure can, of course, be overdone. One fabulously wealthy woman I've visited has pots of roses and perennials brought in from her country estate to be placed in her Manhattan apartment's marble entrance, as if a garden had sprung up from all her marble slabs. The plants, of course, hate it, and have to be sent back to their greenhouse after a week's abuse in the windowless cell. While I sympathize with the lady's craving for plants, the unnaturalness of the setting wouldn't bring me pleasure.

On the other hand, I recall with admiration the way music teacher Victor Nelson turned his small Manhattan terrace into a blooming jungle, overflowing with container-grown plants and trees. It was an unexpected oasis of tropical lushness that provided privacy and beauty in the midst of city buildings, so private and personal that you could imagine yourself deep in the country. Using plant stands, he lifted fragrant flowers to different heights, elevating their fragrance to nose level at the same time as he hid the railings and blocked the view of a busy street. Any plants that grow in a garden can be grown in a container if they are given the root run they need and are watered and fed regularly. They may be easily changed to reflect the season, or allowed to live out their lifespan in the same pot.

Something as simple as planting scented flowers in a window box places them in a spot where the perfume can readily waft in through an open window. Powerfully fragrant long-blooming annuals such as petunias and heliotropes are the best choices. A hanging basket is also an excellent way to place scent at a level where it can more easily be enjoyed: hanging baskets on porches pour out a scented greeting, and hung from trees and lampposts they can be real showstoppers.

Every season, as I look around the gardens, I find new places and ways to add scent. You will too.

Scent is not released from all plants in the same way or with the same intensity. Plants differ greatly, and it is on the basis of these differences that I have organized them into categories for the sake of discussing them.

The first—and the most prominent—group of scented flowers are those I call *seductresses:* heavily perfumed flowers that come out to greet you before you even see them. Seductresses are so important in the fragrant garden that at least one group of them should be in bloom at all times. I have introduced them according to the seasons in which they bloom in my Zone 7 garden. My aim is to help you plan and plant for a succession of them.

At the closing of the eighth century, Charlemagne issued a decree for *lilies* and *roses* (among other plants) to be planted in public gardens.

The next group are the *come-closers:* their fragrance is more subtle, as if to keep their gift of sweetness a secret, sharing it only with those willing to approach closely. Nevertheless, gathered into a bouquet and brought inside, most are strong enough to scent a room. Many come-closers are smaller plants that must be grown in larger numbers (a dozen or more) to make their presence known. I introduce them according to their flowering season, too.

A *moonlighter* disperses perfume from early evening into the night or, if it is also fragrant by day, increases its outpouring of scent in the evening. Moonlighters should be planted to bloom from early summer into fall, when warm evenings are enjoyed in the garden. Most of them are as heavily scented as the seductresses, sending out a fragrant message to pollinators busy after dark, and I plant them in abundance.

Shaggy dogs are plants that hide aromas in their leaves, releasing them only when petted or scratched. Herbs feature prominently here, but you might be surprised to learn about some of the other plants with similar behavior.

Rogues are placed in a chapter by themselves. These plants behave eccentrically as far as scents are concerned. They include the *love-'em-or-hate-'em* varieties, which either appeal or appall, depending on who is smelling them; the *nose twisters*, whose pungent odors require careful handling; the *dual personalities*, which hide unpleasant aromas in their stems or leaves while offering sweet smells from their blossoms; and finally the *stinkers*, whose problem is all too obvious.

2 the seductresses

MY GARDENING BEGAN with an indiscriminate love of flowers, and it has never left me. From the start I wanted both beauty and perfume, which might be regarded as greedy. Yet when I realized that flowers with this combination are the most memorable—the unforgettable ones that poets write about—I knew I was not alone. The father of botany, the Greek historian Theophrastus (ca. 372–ca. 287 B.C.), is credited with the observation that "the best perfumes are made from roses, white lilies, and violets." After more than two thousand years, this remains as true as ever.

Even people uninterested in gardens or gardening know the names of the most famous seductresses of scent: gardenia, hyacinth, lilac, lily, lily-of-the-valley, rose, and tuberose. These species yield perfumes of strength, depth, and complexity. Moreover, their scents are so cunning that they never reveal their makeup all at once; something is always held back for later. They leave you wanting more. But all intensely perfumed flowers have a unique ability to call to us from afar. Most often we smell the fragrance before we see the blossoms, and the perfume invites us to find them, lifting our spirits and making us smile.

Most seductress scents are loud, obvious, very heady, and all-encompassing. There is nothing subtle about the powerful cloud of fragrance they billow into the air. Some can be suffocating, making us feel almost as if we were swimming in perfume. If, as we suppose, their purpose is to attract insects for pollinating, they are leaving nothing to chance.

"Nor is the fragrant garden ever wholly our own. . . . Over hedge or wall, and often far down the highway, it sends a greeting, not alone to us who have toiled for it, but to the passing stranger, the blind beggar, the child skipping to school, the tired woman on her way to work, the rich man, the careless youth."
—LOUISE BEEBE WILDER

15

These heavily scented flowers are the ones that are most needed to set the stage and frame the garden. The trick is to plan so that at least one seductress is in bloom at all times during the gardening season. In this chapter, I deal with them sequentially according to their bloom time in my own garden, though this can of course change depending on the weather.

Unfairly, the tropics are home to more than their share of the earth's strongly scented flowers—they are the very essence of what we think of as a tropical paradise. If you live in a tropical climate, you'll have no problem with fragrance through the seasons. The heavily sweet perfume of the wedding flower *(Stephanotis floribunda)* and the jasminelike scent of the frangipani *(Plumeria alba)* are two of the best known. They haven't grown well for me as houseplants, but if I ever move south, they'll be the first ones I plant. Farther north, away from the tropics, fewer strongly scented flowers exist, but there are always enough to satisfy even me, the greediest gardener. While I envy the southerner for want of warm-blooded frangipani, they in turn must envy me my cold-blooded daffodils.

In planning scented flowers for every season, the farther north you live, the more you will have to rely on houseplants for winter scents. Spring and summer are the easiest seasons to plan and plant for fragrance. Fall continues for a time with the bloom of summer annuals and adds a few flowers all its own. Yet for anyone living with a few months of snow, winter is difficult.

fragrance in the spring garden

Where I live, our gardens are warmed in winter by their proximity to a bay off the Long Island Sound, and cooled by the same bay in the summer. This places us on the edge of Zone 7; only a few miles inland is Zone 6. Our eight

hundred feet of shoreline does not face the open Sound, either, but a protected cove on the mainland, so for us gentle breezes are the norm. (That is, unless a storm is brewing or a hurricane passes our way. Lately, such storms have been a yearly occurrence, bringing the garden season to a rough and sudden close.)

During our first sixteen years, we took mild winters for granted. Snow never stayed on the ground for more than forty-eight hours. Sweet-smelling snowdrops might arrive as early as late December and could be counted on for January cheer. The rest of the spring bulbs and perennials followed placidly, rarely crowding one another, confident in their opportunity to be admired each in its turn.

The last few years I have awakened all too often on a wintry morning with the impression that a genie must have kidnapped and moved us all— husband, kids, dogs, house, and garden—to the outback of Alaska. The first snow in late December seems never to end, as if we have been forgotten for months at a time. Suddenly, in late March the sun shines, warm air breezes in, and the first snowdrops pop up. Just as suddenly other bulbs follow, and the garden erupts in a grand hallelujah. Bulbs that have never seen one another—snowdrops and species tulips—embrace and chorus together.

If I controlled the weather, choosing the pattern would be difficult. Long winters chain my body indoors and take their toll on my moods. But a foreshortened spring can be the most glorious of all with overlaps of bloom bringing a kaleidoscope of changing color. Flowers whose normal bloom time has passed will now bloom helter-skelter with flowers whose time has come. The earliest bulbs may be delayed by up to three months. As we progress through late spring and into summer, the timetable steadies, varying by weeks rather than months. Keep this in mind as you read through my gardener's calendar. At any time of the year, seasons can blend and overlap one with another. No two years are alike.

DAFFODILS

In the fragrant garden, spring really begins with daffodils. Certain of these trumpeters announce the season with a heavy scent, and they are the first bulbs to have their perfume noticed on a cool day. Scentless daffodils are in the majority, however, so choose carefully. I started by planting a thousand bulbs each fall and quickly escalated to five or eight thousand more each year. Although the numbers may sound impressive, a thousand daffs are needed to ring a tree or to make a good showing. Lest you are concerned about all that digging, please note that I plant them closer together than is usually recommended—four to six inches apart. I dig trenches or bucket-sized holes and easily put in a thousand in a couple of hours. Besides, I'm able to spread the planting over three good months—September, October, and November—and if I'm running late I've even managed to sneak in bulbs in December or January.

In the early years, I selected daffodil varieties for their good looks rather than for their scent. Fortunately, many were scented anyway. Later I sought out early and late bloomers to extend the show, and now I only add scented varieties.

With careful selection, it is possible to plant successive scented varieties for a three-month-long display. I learned this the hard way: from my early ignorance and over-planting emerged a succession of scented blooms. The best of the plantings were clusters of Queen Annie's double jonquil *(Narcissus odorus plenus)*, 'Trevithian', and 'Tête-à-Tête' for early bloom; 'Carlton', 'Big Gun', and 'Baby Moon' for midseason; and 'Sir Winston Churchill', 'Yellow Cheerfulness', and 'Thalia' as a finale. These nine daffs include a mix of miniatures ('Baby Moon', 'Tête-à-Tête', and 'Thalia'), doubles (*N. odorus plenus*, 'Sir Winston Churchill', and 'Yellow Cheerfulness'), large-cupped ('Big Gun' and 'Carlton') and flat-cupped ('Trevithian'). Most are sweetly fragrant, and 'Carlton' has a vanilla scent while 'Big Gun' is reminiscent of cotton candy.

Once you've planted so as to assure a full season of fragrant daffodils, supplement with varieties that add unique scents and beauty. Consider the spicy scents of 'Edna Earl', 'Honolulu', and 'Actaea', the pheasant's-eye narcissus. 'Cheerfulness' brings a musky scent, and 'Mondragon' is applelike, while 'Petrel' is a fruit compote.

A Garden of Fragrance

This mix includes three miniatures, but more could be added—I adore miniatures with so many fragrant flowers on short multiple stems. They fit easily in a rock garden, between stepping stones, naturalizing with the primroses, and lending beauty and scent to a low-growing ground cover such as ajuga or grass. On the other hand, the larger doubles are gorgeous. My favorites include 'Erlicheer', 'Cheerfulness', and 'Tahiti'. Naturally, the more petals, the more fragrance.

LILY-OF-THE-VALLEY

Moving forward into the season, lily-of-the-valley has one of the best scents of spring and is especially delightful indoors. A bunch of its sweet-spicy perfumed, waxy white bells will easily scent a room. Lily-of-the-valley is a good woodland or shade plant thriving in leafmoldy, moist situations, easily tucked under the skirts of trees or large shrubs, where it will spread to form an effective ground cover. When it pierces through the cold earth with its leaves scrolled around its flowers, I find myself wondering whether it is only shy or is protecting its scent from the cold, windy dampness of spring.

Out of curiosity, I have planted the pink-flowered lily-of-the-valley, 'Rosea'. It too is powerfully perfumed, but it wears too much rouge, giving it an artificial glow. I find it a garden curiosity rather than a beauty.

HYACINTHS

Hyacinths are always welcome. Their strong scent is reminiscent of a ripe plum pie baked with cloves and topped with cinnamon sugar, and highly complex; if I stay near hyacinths for any length of time, their per-

How an *unseen scent* can move us without force to tears or smiles is a mystery. But there is scientific proof that of all the senses, smell is closest to that part of the brain where memory is stored. Researchers have speculated that this startling associative power is a holdover from the earliest times before we had language, when distinguishing between the smell of a rabbit and a tiger was a matter of life or death.

Today each of us has our own aromatic memories and the fragrance of a flower can call up a long lost memory. A flower's perfume has been called "liquid memory"—a powerful reminder of childhood. Whenever I breathe the perfume of lily-of-the-valley, I remember the bunch of flowers my grandfather brought me from his backyard to take to my kindergarten teacher. As he drove me the short distance to school, I buried my nose in the bouquet. I have never again had as large or as fragrant a bouquet as the one in my memory. Frangipani, too, that heavenly perfume of the tropics, takes me back to my honeymoon on Bali, when I wore a fresh frangipani flower in my hair each day.

fume seems to echo and reverberate, revealing other unidentifiable wisps of scent while withholding the familiar ones. Like other powerful floral perfumes, the scent of hyacinths is deep and composed of many notes.

Visually, I find hyacinths a bit too formal for their own good. They stand apart in mixed company. If there ever was a "black tie" flower, hyacinths would head my list. Their formal bearing and rigidity are difficult to blend with other flowers or shrubs in a garden. Uncomfortably top-heavy, they remind me of overdressed floozies, tottering down a city street on high heels. I don't know how they keep their heads up. Luckily, they relax more each year they return, blooming with fewer flowers on softly curving stems while still retaining their strong scent. As they loosen up they are reverting back to their former selves, before they were hybridized, and that is when I like them best, relaxed and carefree. I clump them together when I plant them in borders to avoid emphasizing their straight backs. Mostly I fill a corner of the vegetable garden with them for cutting; I can leave them there undisturbed for next year's bouquets.

Forced indoors, away from stormy weather, hyacinth stems easily support the full weight of the flower heads and have perfect posture. I prefer to force them in individual hyacinth glasses, not buried in the soil, so I can watch their pointed green noses emerge from their deep purple bulbs. As they stretch, the leaves part, and fully formed flowers dramatically rise as they open.

In the last century, there were hundreds of hyacinth cultivars on the market, and approximately two-thirds of them were doubles. Today a gardener would be hard-pressed to gather one hundred cultivars. Some of my still-available favorites for the sake of their perfume include 'City of Haarlem', a sweetly scented yellow, and the richly perfumed 'L'innocence'.

GARDENIAS, DAPHNES, AND LILACS

As powerfully scented as many spring bulbs are, they can easily be outdone by a fragrant shrub in full bloom. This is especially true of gardenia, daphne, and lilac. I consider the gardenia—*Gardenia jasminoides*, that is (syn. *G. florida*, *G. augusta*)—the uncrowned queen of all fragrant flowers. Each blossom is a regal beauty with thick, milky white petals that overlap like a rose. When a gardenia blooms each spring, it lavishes its rich fragrance upon the breeze and you'll notice little else. Its heavy, floral scent is so powerful that a single blossom can perfume a room. As a cut flower, its ability to last days out of water made it a popular corsage in the days when women regularly wore flowers to dances, weddings, and other special occasions. Unlike most flowers, even as the gardenia petals brown and dry, they continue releasing their perfume. So far as I am concerned, a gardenia on a bedside table is a better get-me-up than the smell of morning coffee. It encourages me to rise happily and shine.

Envy is an acceptable sin in gardeners, because it spurs us on to new accomplishments. I do envy those who live in warmer climates for their seemingly easy culture of gardenias and the large bushes they manage to grow outdoors. In Florida in April I've swooned over an island planting, five feet high and equally wide, of gardenia bushes in full bloom. In California, lucky gardeners may scatter gardenias among their foundation plantings.

For a northern gardener, gardenias are frightfully difficult, especially willful, and cranky when trapped in pots indoors. Still, in spite of its preening and demanding temperament, I have always kept a gardenia in the house. They drive a hard bargain. I have discarded less fussy plants without a backward glance. But not the gardenia. It is the one plant that holds me in its clutches, and I would do backflips to please it. In late spring and early summer, when it blooms in the North, I place it outside in a shady spot where we dine, and it causes no trouble. Winter, when mealybugs and white fly abound, is a different story. Neglect the gardenia for a moment, and its foliage becomes a battlefield. I have lowered my expectations considerably. My goal now is merely to keep it alive through the winter, and I have succeeded, although sometimes just barely. In the summer it recovers and returns to blooming good health.

When I read in the *Wall Street Journal* that gardenias like coffee grounds, I drank more coffee (anything to help my loved ones). I heap coffee grounds regularly around the base of the plant. I don't know that it has helped, but as yet it hasn't hurt. Nevertheless, the moral of the gardenia story must in the end be: Don't get too attached. It flowers mostly when young and can depart at any time.

If it is the heavy sweet scent of *Gardenia jasminoides* that you're after, rather then the beauty of its flowers, there are easier varieties to grow. *Gardenia* 'Prostrata' has smaller, looser petals held in a pinwheel formation. And the African gardenia, *Mitriostigma axillare*, with tiny waxy white flowers, blooms year round. It grows sluggishly but this is in fact an advantage, because it rarely becomes uncomfortable in its pot. Both *Gardenia* 'Prostrata' and the African gardenia are easily grown as houseplants.

Although daphnes are also powerfully scented, they are not as temperamental as the gardenia and need no special care. However, they are short-lived and have a reputation for suddenly departing without notice. A week after *Good Morning America* visited to tape a segment on flowering shrubs, prominently featuring my six-year-old *Daphne caucasica*, it promptly died for no explicable reason. Never during its lifetime did it have a sick day nor was it attacked by garden pests. Daphnes are so valuable for their fragrance, a unique spicy scent, misted with rose perfume and sprinkled with anise, that I have learned to plant a new one every few years as an insurance policy against the current favorite taking flight.

Like gardenias and daphnes, lilacs lavish their fragrance on all that pass. Theirs is a traveling scent, strong yet never overpowering. In my garden they feature most prominently in the lilac and peony walk originally designed by landscape architect Alice Recknagal Ireys fourteen years ago. This S-shaped path stretches between the formal flower garden and the vegetable garden, softly curving twice en route. White lilacs surrounded by white peonies mark each end. Pink lilacs darken to blue and purple in the middle, where pink and red peonies complete the show.

As the path was originally designed, it featured eighteen lilacs planted in three groups of six equally spaced shrubs. Each group of six was equally divided with three on each side of the path. The original group was selected to provide the full range of doubles and singles planted in colors moving from white to soft pinks to blues and purples before fading back to white. Prominent are the cultivars of the common lilac, *Syringa vulgaris*, the strongest scented species of lilacs and the longest blooming (typically from sixteen to twenty days). All have the true lilac scent, the one most prized.

The best among those we chose turned out to be French hybrid cultivars bred in the nineteenth and the beginning of the twentieth centuries in France by the Lemoine family. Many of these classics are more strongly scented and more mildew-resistant than newer ones. *S. vulgaris* 'Miss Ellen Willmott', introduced in 1903, is a very dependable double white bloomer. It has long been considered one of the best of the French hybrids. 'Lucie Baltet' (1888) is a pink single, differing from many lilacs in that it is a low-growing shrub; its coppery buds open into a pale pink. 'President Grevy' (1886) is one of the finest double blues. All four lilacs are midseason bloomers and bloom together. The first peonies start as they are in full bloom.

Several later blooming Chinese lilacs, *S. villosa*, were mixed in the pink section to extend the bloom. Their lavender pink flowers bloom with the mid- and late-blooming peonies into early June. *S. villosa* doesn't have the true lilac scent, but instead has a pleasing musky scent with spicy undercurrents. At the head of the path, peeking over the formal garden wall, is a pink-flowered tree form of the littleleaf lilac, *S. microphylla*. It exhales a light musk and is the last to bloom, so I am let down slowly.

As I've discovered other lilacs, I've deepened the borders, gradually expanding the collection until there are now twenty-nine. I also have tucked another dozen in odd corners of our property so that I can cut branches without disturbing the beauty of the path.

'Miss Kim' is an outstanding cultivar of *S. patula* with a spicy perfume uniquely its own. (Although it was found in the wild in 1895, it wasn't marketed until 1938.) It grows relatively slowly to produce a smaller shrub, without the gangly growth of common lilacs, making it a better choice for smaller spaces. 'Miss Kim' blooms later than the common lilacs, with purple buds opening to single, frosty blue flowers. It has the added attraction of bright fall color, unusual in a lilac, when the leaves glow in shades of mauve and purple.

I must regard the 'Primrose' lilac as a mistake. Shamelessly overmarketed, its "primrose yellow color" is sure to disappoint. No wonder I promptly forgot its name after planting it the summer of 1989. When it bloomed, its lackluster white hue led me to think it was a sickly sucker until I discovered the tag reminding me of my purchase. So I squinted my eyes and looked again. When it first opens and the sun is gleaming on it, it indeed has a slight yellow tint, but nothing to write home about. I should have been tipped off when the catalogs recommended planting it next to a white lilac to appreciate the difference. Its one virtue, if you can call it that, is a scent that reminds me of spicy aftershave.

Certain 'Primrose' lilac strains are better for color: keep an eye out for those marked 'Primrose L' (for a plant from A. Lumley) or 'Primrose H' (connoting a Holden Arboretum selection). Root cuttings from one of these selections will have better color. If you must have one, buy it in bloom so you are sure what you are getting.

The most unusual lilac is also a great beauty. *S. vulgaris* 'Sensation' is appropriately named. Each deep purple petal is ringed with a white halo, and the scent is full-bodied and leaves a sweet trail. 'Sensation' is a must-have.

PEONIES

Since the lilac path wouldn't be half as beautiful without the peonies, I'll introduce them here. Peonies are an old and admirable family, the perfect companion plants for lilacs. Once you've looked into the upturned face of a peony, it is impossible not to want to adopt it. These scene-stealing grande dames have plenty of style and a heart anxious to please. From their first crimson shoots through their full-blown flowers and on to their last bronze-tinged fall foliage, they are gorgeous.

Brought inside, peonies generously waft their perfume through every open doorway. When I fill a vase with a dozen or more peonies and place it in the entrance near the staircase, their fragrance is easily detected in adjoining rooms and remarkably floats up the staircase to the second and third floors as well.

Their longevity is only one of their blessings. They know their place in the garden and remain without squawking until divided. (While root cuttings of lilacs are variable, incidentally, divisions of peonies produce exact replicas.)

Breeders classify three distinct scents in peonies—rose, honey, and an unpleasant odor that's reminiscent of soap and bitter medicine. The evil smell is associated with the pollen-bearing cultivars, and this makes the red singles the worst offenders. 'America', however, is a red single that is an exception to the rule and boasts a lightly sweet breath. I have a clump growing where it is visible from the lilac and peony walk. In many singles and semidoubles, the pungent smell of the pollen can at times overcome the otherwise sweet fragrance of the petals. The good news is that the off odor of the pollen does not travel, and can be smelled only when you bend and put your nose inside the blooms. In general, fully double rose type peonies are the most fragrant. Single peonies are generally lacking in scent or ill-scented.

When it came to selecting my peonies, I had dumb luck. Of the original eight cultivars of peonies we planted, all were old-fashioned classics, all fragrant, and all but one on a recommended list for commercial cut-flower production (see the plant portrait chapter, page 115). I've noted in parentheses the year the cultivar was born for two reasons. First, they make me feel young; second, any plant that has retained its popularity for a century or more is not to be sneezed at.

'Festiva Maxima' (1851), already in the garden when we bought the house, has large bowls of double white flowers that are uniquely splashed in the center with flecks of red, making it easy to identify. It is the first peony along the walk to bloom, and its scent reminds some people of a rose (to me it smells like sweet talcum powder). 'Festiva Maxima' starts the walk among white lilacs at the entrance to the vegetable garden and is a counterpart to 'Baroness Schroeder', planted near the white lilacs at the far end, at the entrance to the formal garden. 'Baroness Schroeder' (1889) has rose-shaped double white flowers faintly tinged with pink, and is a late bloomer. Late bloomers are not plentiful, and the peony season is short, so I cherish the ones I find to help me prolong the season.

I didn't realize it at the time, but planting the walk with lilacs and peonies was just the beginning. Gardens evolve, and one scented flower makes me yearn for another. So what started as a lilac and peony walk became a path planted with scented blooms of many other kinds, fragrant for nine months of the year. All that is missing, in fact, is winter bloom—and that is not needed here because the walk is rarely frequented in winter.

Looking for ways to extend the scent and beauty, I decided to plant three tree peonies. Tree peonies are different from the typical herbaceous ones; they have woody stems that don't die back to the ground in winter and they grow almost as wide as they grow tall—ultimately reaching four feet. Their extra-large flowers, often the size of salad plates, are a marvel of engineering. Their petals can be crinkled like crepe paper or silken and translucent with the look of fine porcelain. Few flowers figure as prominently in Oriental art as these beauties. I rationalize picking most of the flowers just as they open to spare them the torrents of spring wind and rains. Indoors, away from harm, they live longer and their breathtaking beauty can be admired more.

Breeders praise two distinct scents in tree peonies—the lemon scent found in *P. lutea* and the sweet and yeasty musk scent of *P. suffruticosa*. However, I have yet to smell any tree peony whose fragrance I really like when I put my nose in the bloom. Still, the beauty of their flowers and the delicate soft scent they float in the air makes them easy to accept.

So I placed the tree peonies 'Guardian of the Monastery', 'Hephestos', and an unnamed yellow midway in the walk to bloom before the lilacs, and often they stay to greet their arrival and blend their sweet scents. 'Guardian of the Monastery' has huge blooms, averaging ten inches across. The semidouble layers of crinkled petals are cream with wide swaths of lavender melting into raspberry flares running down the middle of each petal as they radiate out from a golden mount of stamen. 'Hephestos' is the only double tree peony I grow, and its flowers are slightly smaller than 'Guardian of the Monastery'. It is a deep ruby red with pointed and ruffled petals. The nameless yellow is not as showy, with single flowers closer to six inches across, but it is more prolific and the smaller blooms are not as fragile. I mostly leave them on the bush to be enjoyed in the garden.

After a year or two I realized that the path looked a little bare early in the season before the lilacs leafed out and the peonies showed their faces. So I planted clusters of daffodils and Siberian squill under the bare branches of the lilacs. The bulbs have naturalized under and between the lilacs and refused to be crowded out by the shrubs' increasing girth. A strip of grass between the brick path and the lilac bed became a problem to mow, so out it came, to be replaced by lightly sweet-scented St. John's-wort *(Hypericum calycinum)*, which blooms in midsummer and sporadically into the late fall. The green leaves turn reddish brown after a prolonged cold spell, but they stay on the stems until I give them a haircut in late winter, just before the new growth starts. The original narrow strip of St. John's-wort has crept back between the peonies and scooted under the lilacs to knit the path together. A southern magnolia, *Magnolia grandiflora*, adds a vertical to one curve in the path and blares a loud and heady sweet scent in the hot and humid days of summer. A couple of daphne extend the bloom season. *Daphne genkwa*, the lilac daphne with a light scent, blooms first each year, sometimes in March, most often in April. The Caucasian daphne, *D. caucasica*, starts bloom in April and doesn't stop until November or December. It is strongly scented. I don't know a more generous shrub.

Fragrant trees, the Johnny-come-latelies to the path, drench the air with their perfume. I've always approached gardening from the wrong direction—planting flowers before the trees. Now I'm making up for lost time. On one side a tall yellow wood *(Cladrastis lutea)* blooms ten feet from the path in May, and anyone in the area smells the pronounced vanilla scent—with deep notes of hyacinth—from its pendulous ropes of white pealike flowers. Then the rambling rose 'Seagull' climbs its trunk, and blossoms tumble down from its bottom branches for three weeks in June after the lilacs and peonies have finished. I've bottom-pruned the rose to three stems and trained them to follow the trunk to the first limb, and from there they are all on their own to branch out and seek the sun. A nearby flowering Bradford pear, planted long before the path existed, claims the sweet vanilla scent of the small white flowers of *Clematis montana* living in its branches as its own. Fair enough— after all, they are dependent on each other.

FRAGRANT SHRUBS

The three goddesses of late spring and early summer are Korean spice viburnum *(Viburnum carlesii)*, with its broad, flat heads of spicy-scented white flowers; the perfumed small white bells of the mock orange *(Philadelphus* x *lemoinei* 'Innocence'); and the flaming orange-red single flowers of the Japanese flowering quince *(Chaenomeles japonica)*, which combines the scent of a fruit tart and the smell of honey. (A bowl of its small quinces will perfume a room as they dry and shrivel.) All of these shrubs thrive in some shade, so it was not difficult to find a place for them under the canopy of a tree or next to a building. The Korean spice viburnum is at the entrance to the drive, the mock orange grows as a hedge connecting the oak trees along the driveway, and the flowering quince is by my back door. I had placed them to screen out the neighbors and the cars that drive by without realizing I would pass them each day and be captivated by their scent as I come and go from the house to check the mailbox. Once I realized how often I passed them, I underplanted each with daffodils that bloom at the same time so their beauty and scent are enhanced.

There are, of course, other viburnums, mock oranges, and flowering quinces that carry wonderful scents, and if room permits, they are great garden plants. And there are dozens of fragrant flowering shrubs. For example, the Carolina allspice, also known as the sweet shrub, *Calycanthus floridus*, is widely appreciated. Its flowers are more curious than beautiful: each is chestnut brown and cone-shaped, with petals curving inward rather than opening wide at the mouth, as if masquerading as last year's seedpods. Their fragrance has been noted—though with little unanimity—by many garden writers. According to Ken Druse, the sweet shrub "reeks like the inside of a whisky barrel." The Wayside catalog claims it "smells like strawberries," while at least one book calls it "bubble gum scented." William H. Frederick, Jr., in *The*

Exuberant Garden, finds it "a cross between bananas and strawberries," and remains enthusiastic: "There should be a plant of calycanthus near the entrance to every house, as this fragrance is a very important part of the voluptuousness with which early May assaults our shrunken winter senses."

I agree with Frederick about the attractiveness of Carolina allspice. Perhaps some of the confusion about its fragrance can be explained by the fact that it is triple-scented: its flowers have one scent, the fruity scent of ripe apples or (some say) pineapple; the leaves, wood, and roots have a powerful camphor aroma; and the bark smells and tastes so much like cinnamon that it has been used as a cinnamon substitute.

Blooming a little later, and not as often seen, is the native American fringetree *(Chionanthus virginicus)*, one of the largest shrubs, reaching twenty feet at maturity and often mistakenly called a tree. A pair of them standing on my front lawn is a lovely sight; the white spangles of sweet-scented flowers can be admired even from a distance. And spring is not its only season of beauty. If there is a male shrub nearby, the female bears deep blue grape-size ornamental fruit in late summer. The fruits are beautiful dangling against the bright yellow foliage if they are not too quickly consumed by the birds. No wonder it was a favorite of Thomas Jefferson, who grew it at Monticello.

Vines too can be powerfully scented. The ever-popular Chinese wisteria, *W. sinensis,* has faintly fragrant, lilac-blue, pea-shaped flowers that hang in pendulous clusters almost a foot long. The Japanese wisteria, *W. floribunda,* and its hybrid *W. formosa* are the most fragrant wisteria, more so than the American *W. frutescens. W. venusta* is only slightly scented. 'Kuchi Beni', 'Longissima alba', 'Ivory Tower', 'Macrobotrys', 'Naga Noda', and 'Rosea', all cultivars of *W. floribunda,* are some of the best varieties to grow for fragrance.

But remember that a newly planted wisteria is slow to bloom. Seven years is not unusual. More important, it can be over-bearing in its later years. Its serpentine habit and boa constrictor strength need close watching. The best and most prolific bloom comes when the vines are pruned back monthly during the summer growing season, stopping in September before the following year's flower buds are formed. Pruned as a standard or a craggy tree, wisteria's undisciplined behavior is kept in check and its beauty remains flawless. On our house, pruning is mandatory several times a year, since we value our roof. To play it safe, we attached a wooden beam to the outside of our house, below the second-story windows, to hold two wisteria, one on each side. One mild winter day, after the vines had grown for a few years and were still flexible, we detached the long, twelve-foot stems from the house, laid them on the ground, and removed the weak, thin stems, leaving three main stems on each vine. We pruned away the lower leaves up to eight feet high, in order to train the vines to branch above the porch at the second story. Then we braided the main stems, just as I braid my daughter's hair. It took two of us to braid them, a May dance of sorts, as we stepped up and over one stem, and crawled under another while holding on to the third. When we finished, the braided stems were lifted up and retied to the beam. As the years have passed, the braid has increased in girth and the foliage and flowers swag from the beam under the windows as we intended.

The common wallflower, *Cheiranthus cheiri*, is no trouble, though as a biennial it needs to be seeded each summer for the next spring blooms. Unhappily, it disappears when hot weather arrives. But seeded one summer on our seaside bank, it prolifically reseeded itself in both sun and shade and flowered for many years before the combination of a high tide and a ravaging wind washed it out to sea. Wallflowers are deliciously anise-scented, especially the yellow and mahogany-colored cultivars. They bloom in clusters of one-inch, four-petaled flowers topping each stem, resembling smaller, shorter garden phlox. In England, the twelve-inch varieties are a traditional favorite for underplanting tulips.

An eighteen-inch yellow wallflower is a great companion for the lilac-colored blooms of the dame's rocket, *Hesperis matronalis*, another self-sowing biennial, happy in most situations to spritz its clove fragrance several yards away. If they are allowed to flower together, their colors complement each other and their rich strong perfumes blend and jostle in the wind. Their appearance too is similar although dame's rocket is twice as tall and more relaxed in its growth. The dame's rocket steps gently around our yard, planting a few seedlings here and there for next year's blooms. It is always reluctant to leave, blooming for more than two months, although it looks tattered and torn as it completes its cycle. In prominent places I pull it up before it finishes. In the wilder gardens and the cutting garden it departs on its own.

Trees too have their fair share of fragrant flowers. First to come to mind is an orchard of orange blossoms. I have smelled them in bloom while miles away from the orchard. But that was in Florida. I console myself with a small potted *Citrus limon* 'Meyer's Lemon' that grows in a sunny window and can be depended on in late winter to perfume the house. The whole plant is scented from its leaves to its fruit and flowers.

The small flowers of the large European linden, *Tilia platyphyllos*, have a wonderful sweet honey scent that floats unpredictably on the air, taunting and teasing me. There are times when the flowering linden withholds its scent even to someone standing under its limbs. Yet from far across the lawn I have been reminded of its presence by fragrance.

fragrance in the summer garden
Among the summer bulbs, a single powerfully perfumed Oriental lily can scent a garden while a clump of them may send a greeting over the hedge or wall, around corners and often far down the block. When lilies are in bloom, all other fragrances pale: their perfume catches the passerby and makes him look back to admire the flower's beauty. No manmade perfume ever smelled so good. Yet there are distinctions to be made here too: the regal lily, *Lilium regale*, has a perfume similar to honeysuckle, while that of the Easter lily, *L. longiflorum*, is more like jasmine.

Lilies are easy to tuck into gardens, under shrubs, between perennials, and at the back of flower borders. Since lilies grow straight up on a single, scantily clad stem, they take up very little room. And the bulbs are deeply planted—usually six to eight inches deep—so they leave space for other plants

The Seductresses

above. Luckily, lilies prefer to have their ankles shaded by the skirts of other plants, while their heads grow in the sun. If they are partnered with full-bodied perennials and shrubs, the lilies won't need staking. Lupines, balloon flowers, roses, and vitex are all obliging supports for the lilies in my garden.

Normally I'm pretty conventional and put lilies where their height is in keeping with their neighbors', but every now and then I've thrown convention to the wind, staggering a half dozen near the front of a border or standing above a shorter ground cover. The lilies appear as if they're all dressed up and out for a stroll. I've learned there isn't a wrong place to plant lilies—they bring beauty and grace with them wherever they go.

My preference is for lilies with large outwardly facing trumpets rather than ones that look up. 'Golden Splendor' is a Chinese trumpet, true to its name. It stands four feet or more above the annual garden at the pool and I've never disturbed it with my yearly planting nor has it ever needed staking. When planted at the back of the border, 'Black Beauty' is obvious—if not for its height, then for its face paint. It has deep crimson petals penciled with a white outline. The petals are drawn back like a bow, perhaps to send its fragrance flying from its imperial height of nine feet. More prolific than most, it becomes nearly shrublike when mature and, if happy in its garden site, can send out more than fifty flowers. (See more about lilies in the plant portraits, page 125.)

Bearded iris too can be strongly sweet-scented. There are thousands of iris cultivars available in the trade today, and new ones are being introduced yearly: a sweetly fragrant bearded variety is easy to find. 'Banbury Ruffles', 'Beverly Sills', 'Lake Placid', 'Pacific Panorama', and 'Vanity' are some that I am familiar with. Note that the perfume of the iris family is highly variable, however, ranging from scentless to sweet and pleasant to sickeningly sweet-scented, as in grape Kool-Aid.

I find it hard to design bearded iris into a garden. Their bloom is short, from a few minutes in hot weather to two weeks if the weather cooperates, with cool temperatures and no hard rains. I compromised by planting bearded iris in large clumps along a path where no one lingers (unless they're in bloom), next to a pond and on a bank where their short bloom is noticed in season, but doesn't matter the rest of the year. I often pick an iris as they come into bloom to perfume the living room.

The tender summer hyacinth, *Galtonia candicans*, is less formal than the spring hyacinth. Its scent is similar, its stem taller, and it blooms longer, often for a month. From each two-and-a-half-foot stem, twenty to thirty white, green-tinged, bell-shaped flowers loosely dangle above the graceful loops of strap-shaped leaves. I informally cluster them in a narrow flower border near the swimming pool so their scent is easily noticed and I can then remember to dig them up to winter over indoors. As cut flowers they excel, because when the stems are placed in water their scent is stronger.

Among the summer-blooming bulbs, *Crinum* x *powellii* stands out both for its height and sweetness. Its trumpet-shaped flowers topping four-foot stems spritz a far-reaching sweetness akin to that of the sweet violet. I planted several at the back of the formal flower border under the out-stretched branch of a sycamore tree. With only a half day of sun, they bloom from mid-June into September. The bulbs are shallowly planted so their necks are at soil level and each spring I find mushy bulbs protruding. Two years in a row I've assumed I've lost them only to discover them more floriferous than they were the year before. They increase and multiply annually.

The magic lily, *Lycoris squamigera*, named for Mark Anthony's mistress, a beautiful Roman actress, is a late-summer seductress with a spicy scent. In August, six to eight flared trumpets shimmering in lilac appear on leafless stems. Its nicknames—naked lady and resurrection lily—emphasize its leafless stems and quick growth at summer's end. Earlier in the summer, flowerless straps of leaves appear to linger for a few weeks before dying to the ground. A stranger might mistake the leaves for overfed plants refusing to bloom. They easily fit in the middle of a sunny border between perennials, in

front of rosebushes or along a shady walk between hosta as I saw them growing in the Adirondacks. I was surprised that they naturalized in so much shade. The other popular family members, *L. radiata* and *L. sanguinea*, are entirely devoid of scent.

I almost admitted defeat after planting a dozen magic lilies, four at a time, three years in a row when none of them showed their heads above the ground. Then I'd see them in another garden and lust would cloud my thinking. My last attempt proved successful. I have three that flower in the sunny border by the kitchen door. In truth, my soil is too heavy for their taste. They like to stay fairly dry and warm for most of the summer and resent having been moved. Even when happy in their new situation, these headstrong bulbs often refuse to bloom for a year.

ROSES

What would summer be without the roses? No one disputes that roses are the world's most popular flowers. For centuries they've been loved for their beauty, revered for their scent. As described by Louise Beebe Wilder in *The Fragrant Path*, the true old-rose scent, "the scent that has charmed humanity from time immemorial, is assuredly the most exquisite and refreshing of all floral odors—pure, transparent, incomparable—an odor into which we may, so to speak, burrow deeply without finding anything coarse or bitter, in which we may touch bottom without losing our sense of exquisite pleasure." The old-rose fragrance originated with the damask roses and is found today in 'Fashion', 'Gertrude Jekyll', 'Madame Hardy', 'Mary Rose', 'Penelope', 'The Reeve', 'Othello', and 'The Squire', among other roses.

'Madame Hardy' is my favorite damask-scented rose. When covered with flowers she sends her perfume far afield, an open invitation to admire her beauty. She is magnificent alone or planted as an ornamental shrub. Don't be deterred because she blooms only once; she gives oh-so-much more in a single burst than most repeat-blooming roses. Place her in a mixed foundation planting, in a shrub border, or as anchor to a garden seat—anywhere that any other once-blooming shrub would command attention.

Roses do not all smell the same. Their perfumes are a mix of fragrances that have been compared to anise, fruits, herbs, honey, licorice, medicine, myrrh, nasturtiums, spices, tea, and violets. And many a rose scent is so evasive and unique that it can be described only as sweet.

Fourteen years ago, we planted a formal rose garden with ninety hybrid teas, two grandiflora, four polyantha, and six shrub roses. As a dutiful rosarian I sprayed weekly, waging war on every attacking insect—Japanese beetles, aphids, rose midge, you name it. Some days the smell of chemicals hung so heavy in the air, I couldn't smell the roses. Despite my ministering to their every whim, as a group they didn't look good by midsummer and I felt a bit like a nurse in a plague ward.

A decade ago, something clicked. I had completely ceased to believe in the safety of garden chemicals. At a conference I met a rosarian who had neglected to wear protective clothing while spraying her roses and burned her skin. I later learned rosarians in charge of spraying at the New York Botanical Garden are required to have a blood test every six months. If professionals were that worried about pesticides, I concluded, they had no place at my home with four kids, two dogs, two cats, and a fish-filled pond. Not to mention a well from which we all drink the water.

I went cold turkey on the chemicals. But I found that I didn't have to give up on roses. In fact, I've increased their numbers to almost four hundred. The shrub roses, old roses, and climbers casually planted around the grounds look better with less food and water and no chemical sprays than the hybrid teas ever did. Over the next few years, deprived of chemicals, many hybrid teas departed on their own. Others were thrown out with the trash. Two 'Queen Elizabeth' grandiflora roses held court standing regally, one at each side of the crescent garden. I hadn't the heart to prune them within an inch of their lives as is so often recommended, and now they are glorious towers of bloom and scent. Theirs is a woodsy perfume, a combination of wet moss, ferns, and sweetness. With the hybrid teas gone, I've filled up the rose garden

Cultivation of *roses* dates back about five thousand years in China. Just before the birth of Christ, the Han dynasty had huge parks devoted to roses. The parks grew roses even when food was scarce and agricultural lands were needed to feed the population.

The Seductresses
35

with English, shrub, and antique roses. The English include 'Abraham Darby' (strong sweet scent), 'Constance Spry' (myrrh), 'Gertrude Jekyll' (old rose), 'Graham Thomas' (tea), 'Heritage' (sweet with a hint of lemon), 'Mary Rose' (damask and old rose), and two—'L.D. Braithwaite' and 'Lillian Austin'—whose fragrance escapes description. Among the antique roses are 'Souvenir de la Malmaison' (spicy apple) and 'Madame Isaac Pereire' (raspberry).

On a bank by the swimming pool and at the sunny end of the tennis court I've planted more old favorites known for their beauty and scent—'Ballerina', 'Belle de Crecy', 'Charles de Mills', 'Cornelia', 'Fantin Latour', 'Ferdinand Pichard', 'Reine des Violettes', and 'Rosa Mundi.' It was some years after we moved here before I noticed that the red rose growing on our ivy-clad carriage house was using the ivy as a trellis. Seeing that the ivy and rose had entered in a happy marriage, their lives intertwined and compatible for forty years or more, I went ahead and added other roses—'Golden Showers' and 'America'—to the ménage. They are now climbing the ivy too, sprinkling fragrance and lifting the mood in the courtyard garden immeasurably.

After I saw roses climbing trees at Rayford Reddell's Garden Valley Ranch in California I raced out to buy ramblers for my trees. As it turned out, my haste was not matched by the ramblers. I needn't have hurried. Roses take their time clambering aloft. It takes several years and considerable guidance from the gardener to get them into the lower branches from which they can move out on their own.

A small tree can support a shade-tolerant rose such as *Rosa* 'Zephirine Drouhin' with its fruity and clove scent (a raspberry scent jumps out at me, but others call it apple). This remarkable old Bourbon rose, introduced in 1868, blooms all summer with as little as three hours of sun a day. It is also unique for its colorful new growth. Both its stems and leaves stay dark burgundy throughout the summer, unlike many roses where the newborn leaves open red but change to green within a few weeks. Even when flowers are few, the contrasting green and dark red stems and foliage are quite an eye-popping sight. I tie a couple of wires to the tree's lower branches and then attach each to its own peg, driven squarely into the ground near the base of the rose. Once

the rose is ensconced in the tree branches, it no longer needs the wires, nor my guidance. Pruning is a nonissue; it is allowed to wander freely.

I have learned to view the sweetly fragrant multiflora roses climbing some of the trees in the wild part of our garden with greater sympathy. The birds plant them everywhere—I have even pulled them out of the raised vegetable beds. When we first moved in, I cursed them; they seemed ready to take over everywhere, crowding out other plants as they dispersed runners in all directions. Each runner sent up a new bush and the stems climbed on their own, hooking their thorns on the trunk and on branches as they grew. No wires or trellis for them.

I'm still not prepared to accept multifloras just anywhere, but I'm ready to forgive the one growing up the tulip tree. In spring the roses' white flowers cover the long-reaching stems, as if a fluffy cloud of perfume and beauty has been caught among the tree's branches to send down a sweet scent. I have always loved its fall red hips for arrangements, so now I try to be thankful that I can pick them at home instead of along the roadsides.

We now have roses climbing everywhere. The gazebo by the tennis court wears whites when *Rosa* 'Bobby James' blooms. His long arms reach over and around the gazebo to capture and hold the scent closely for those sitting on the sidelines. 'America' is a repeat double salmon rose that sweetly perfumes one end of the grape arbor, and 'Veilchenblau', a unique rose, climbs with thornless stems to freely cast its fruity fragrance from the middle of the arbor everywhere. Although it only blooms once a summer, it's unlike any other rose, with original tie-dyed color, somewhere between purple, violet, and lavender. Each small double blossom is white-eyed and snuggles next to another to bloom in showy clusters. 'Cecile Brunner', the sweetheart rose, climbs the back of the formal flower border and drapes its long limbs over the second-story balcony of the children's playhouse. It too is a one-of-a-kind character, easily recognized for its miniature pink buds,

"The proper way to *smell a rose* is to take the bloom in the hand well up under the neck, bury the nose deep into its very heart and then smell gently, breathing in and out a bit harder than normally just as you would sip a hot drink. It is not necessary to bruise the bloom but do not be afraid to get the nose down into it."

—George W. Forrest

pointed and perfectly formed, that open into double blossoms. This is the reason it was designated and sold as the boutonniere flower. On a post by the playhouse porch is a large-flowered, delicate pink climber, 'Mme. Gregoire Staechelin'; in early summer she breathes her sweet-pea breath on all who sit on the porch, and in fall her red hips hang like baubles. I planted 'New Dawn', a light pink rose with an apple scent, on the pillar at the sunny end of our porch, thinking it would be happy to twine around it and sweetly scent the terrace. It shot like a rocket for the balcony above, which adjoins my bedroom. As the canes scramble over the railing, they lay flowers outside my balcony door. They are the first things I see when I wake each summer morning.

On the arbor at the entrance to the orchard, 'Don Juan', 'Kathleen', and 'Zephirine Drouhin' embrace one another. 'Don Juan' is a favorite with the ladies, and I admit I am susceptible to his charms and powerful perfume. The petals are dark red, velvety, and powerfully perfumed, although I can't describe the scent. (These are the rose petals I toss in a salad, or candy to decorate a cake. They are very sweet and flavorful.) I realize he is a climbing hybrid tea, a leftover guest from my first rose garden, but I don't want to be without him. The two roses with which he is partnered grow more vigorously, covering his branches, so I've never noticed black spot or powdery mildew, and I can always find a powerfully scented red rose to pick. 'Kathleen' is a softly fragrant musk rose whose scent blends easily with her powerfully perfumed companions.

Even the arbors in our vegetable and herb garden have been planted with climbing roses. The entrance was planted first with 'New Dawn', which we liked so much that the next year we planted other roses on the back arbor, sheltering a garden seat. Without too much regard for color (it was the spring rush), we simply planted our favorites for beauty and scent: pink 'Aloha', yellow 'Golden Showers', red 'Don Juan', and multicolored 'Joseph's Coat'. They clash as they climb, but rather than change them, we named the garden seat the "electric chair" for the jolt of color and fragrance you get when you sit on it.

When choosing roses, keep in mind that the newer hybrids often have larger flowers in a broader range of colors, but beware of black sheep that entirely lack perfume (see page 135). My philosophy, as should be obvious by

now, is to grow fragrant roses everywhere and anywhere. I won't accept restraint. More is always better. Can I live by roses alone? Maybe not, but as Dorothy Parker once said, "They that have roses never need bread."

SCENTED PERENNIALS

While a scented garden wouldn't be complete without a rosebush, scented perennials are the staples of a fragrant border. The hosta family is not known for its perfume, but some of my favorite scents blare from the trumpets of a few of them—the descendants or crosses of the only scented species, *Hosta plantaginea*. Unlike the more popular hostas, whose leaves are puckered or quilted, variegated with silver or gold edges, or solid gold or silver-blue, *H. plantaginea*, when not in bloom, are dowdy in appearance, plain Janes that are often overlooked until the end of August. It is then, when most flowers are finishing and the garden is quieter, that *H. plantaginea's* hidden talents shine—or rather, smell. Its cultivars, the larger flowered 'Royal Standard' and the double-trumpeted 'Aphrodite', are favorites of mine. Their white trumpet flowers blare a lilylike perfume, commanding us to pay attention. Cut for a bouquet, their good looks and powerful perfume might lead you to mistake them for white lilies. 'Fragrant Blue' is the first blue-leaved fragrant hosta and it carries a high price tag; I'll wait a few years until it is more reasonably priced. 'Sweetie' is a variegated cultivar with apple green leaves outlined with wide creamy margins, and a lighter scent. Other less fragrant yet still desirable hosta family members include 'Honeybells', 'So Sweet', 'Summer Fragrance', and 'Fragrant Bouquet'. I plant hosta to ring a tree or a shrub, providing a shady ground cover, and clumped into the shady end of our formal flower border.

FRAGRANT ANNUALS

A yearly addition of fragrant annuals rounds out a summer garden. Sweet peas are the best and the most powerfully sweet-scented of all the annuals. They have the depth and complexity of an orange blossom with a pinch of vanilla, a twist of old rose, and a sweetness all their own. Their reputation has been damaged by rumors of temperamental behavior and short bloom time; I find this unfair and feel strongly that it doesn't have to be so. There are new heat-tolerant varieties of sweet pea that bloom longer, and I have learned a few tricks about how to grow the old-fashioned varieties (see page 121). Let's start a revival. Their fragrance is so good that if they were grown in every yard or even on every block, together we could raise the spirits of the entire country.

Another annual known for its intense fragrance but never for its beauty is mignonette *(Reseda odorata)*. A lowly roadside weed, mignonette began its rise to fame when Napoleon Bonaparte sent seed from Egypt to Empress Josephine. Its strong perfume may be compared to the sweetness of ripe raspberries and violets. Josephine grew it as a potted plant to scent the musty rooms at her estate, La Malmaison. As it was fashionable for the ladies of Josephine's court to follow her example, mignonette (French for "little darling") became all the rage. Its popularity as a pot plant lasted until the mid-nineteenth century, when it moved outdoors to be grown mostly as a field flower for the Paris cut-flower market.

While the French adored the strongly scented mignonette, some English gardening books went so far as to claim that its odor was too powerful to be in the home. Instead it was considered the perfect flower for London balconies, where its "breath of garden air" would mask the offensive smells of the streets. Legends accumulated around the plant: Select Seeds, a catalog specializing in heirloom flowers, notes that "a lover who rolls three times in a bed of mignonette will be attended by success, and as it was also employed to treat bruises, a clumsy suitor would at least find the restorative herb conveniently close by!"

Changing taste has driven mignonette into oblivion, and I have never seen it sold as a cut flower. Where mignonette fields once grew, lavender has been planted. But mignonette is still available as seed from many specialty houses, so give it a try. Avoid the hybrid, darker brick colors; they have no scent. The cultivar 'Paris Market', with its greenish brown flowers, tends toward a mustard scent.

In some parts of the country, the common name of heliotrope *(Heliotropium arborescens)* is "cherry pie." Its

Hippocrates, the father of medicine, said, "The way to health is to have an aromatic bath and scented massage every day."

scent reminds me more of vanilla flavoring. One garden writer describes its scent as "vanilla with a dash of cinnamon," while another complains of its "almost sickly almond scent." It is a scent I like, and I grow heliotrope in pots outdoors in the summer so I can move it indoors for the winter. Its clusters of small deep purple flowers easily combine with almost any other color, especially loud annual colors that need bringing down a peg. Though it's sold as an annual, it is a tender perennial. In my greenhouse it blooms year-round, and I can cut the flowers to add scent to small arrangements in winter when fragrant flowers are few.

Ten-week stock, *Matthiola incana*, is much changed from the original little dusty-leaved, craggy plant first found growing in rocky outcroppings high above the Mediterranean. Its spicy sweetness, a penetrating clove perfume, has been inherited by singles and has been increased in the doubles. (Incidentally I am told that the more fragrant doubles can be identified as seedlings by their lighter shade of green.) 'Beauty of Nice', a cultivar growing to thirty inches, is lovely in the front of a border, while 'Mammoth Excelsior', a three-foot-high selection, is excellent for cutting. Stock sold by florists are long-legged beauties of blossom-packed spikes and more pronounced perfume than the popular garden varieties. I grow stock in a cutting garden and only occasionally in a flower border. It is another straitlaced garden flower, yet in arrangements it is unbeatable.

MAGNOLIAS

The blossoms of southern and saucer magnolias (*Magnolia grandiflora* and *M.* x *soulangeana*) are not only powerfully scented but among the most visible, balancing like oversized teacups on the branches. I have two *M. grandiflora* that brave the northern winters, though they don't begin to compare in beauty or size to southern-grown magnolias. Still, one of its foot-sized flowers makes a centerpiece on a dinning table and as it lasts a day or two out of water, it is a good last-minute flower to pick and set in its place.

Standing near a southern magnolia in bloom, the scent has at different times reminded me of lily-of-the-valley, jasmine, and citrus. If I put my nose in the flower I find an unpleasant afterscent trailing its sweetness. Henry Mitchell, the prolific and marvelously opinionated *Washington Post* columnist, also found the matter thoroughly complicated: "The fragrance of *Magnolia grandiflora*," he wrote, "is both obvious and overrated. It is powerful enough to scent an ordinary room if the windows are closed and is agreeable enough, with an undertone of turpentine and an overlay of lemon. It is not at all sweet in the way that night jasmine, tuberoses, gardenias, or regal lilies are."

Another favorite is the sweet bay magnolia *(M. virginiana)*, with its smaller, two-to-three-inch single white blossoms, each a whirl of nine to twelve petals. Its scent reminds me of lemonade, not sweet bay leaves. Although it is never abundantly clothed in flowers as other spring bloomers, its first bloom connects spring to summer and lasts for almost six weeks. As often as not, a few flowers stagger in during the heat of summer, blooming sporadically until September.

Japanese stewartia *(Stewartia pseudocamellia)* is an exceptional tree, slowly growing to maturity at twenty to forty feet. Its sweetly perfumed, two-inch, camellialike flowers bloom in July when few trees flower. The waxy white petals open to reveal stamens of spun gold. Whole flowers drop from the tree at their most beautiful, before they brown to carpet the ground. I find stewartia at its best when half-dressed in summer, but this is a tree for all seasons. It dazzles the eye with brilliant fall foliage in maroon, orange, and yellow, and its decorative bark—mottled with gray, brown, and orange—is a winter and spring attraction.

fragrance in the fall garden
In most gardens, summer's end is the season least planned and planted. Yet with a bit of forethought you can say good-bye to summer with a whoop and a holler instead of a whine.

Some summer annuals linger on to give fall a head start. While a few of the more tenderhearted flee at the first teasing frost in mid-October, other more tenacious bloomers stay until defeated by strong winds and prolonged frost. This is the season, too, for support from some of the powerfully per-

fumed Moonlighters (see page 61), among them petunias, scented nicotianas, daturas, four o'clocks, and moonflowers.

In the cool nights of September, roses rebound from their summer slump. Bloom may be full, but the flower size will probably be smaller than in June. Some roses (for example, 'Blush Nosette', a late bloomer with a sweet tea breath) will still present a few clusters of small double flowers for me to bring into the house as late as early December. 'Eden' is a gorgeous climber that seductively drapes her arms along the top of the swimming pool fence and is one of the last to leave the party. Each flower is a goblet of rosy pink petals trimmed with sparkling white satin. As the flower ages, the outer petals relax and the inner petals blush softly. The perfume 'Eden' pours out is tea stirred with damask. Other roses blooming long into fall are two English roses, 'Graham Thomas', a burning yellow, and 'Mary Rose', a hot pink. Even if heavy frost comes early, I can still salvage many rosebuds for dried flower arrangements.

The *Rosa rugosa* 'Alba' on our beach look their best with both white single flowers harboring golden centers and orange-red hips as big as cherry tomatoes hanging side by side. Their spicy scent is undiminished by cool weather. 'Hansa', a double-flowered magenta rugosa with a stronger clove scent, is only slightly more beautiful than these wildlings.

There are many choice end-of-summer fragrant flowering shrubs. Conni Cross, a garden designer and nursery owner, remembers her first encounter with harlequin glorybower *(Clerodendrum trichotomum)*. "It found me," she says, "one August as I was walking in the Brooklyn Botanic Garden. I was thirty or forty feet away and I couldn't figure out where the fragrance was coming from until one of the staff pointed out a small shrub." In flower and fruit, glorybower is beautiful, with numerous clusters of white starry flowers. It is not unusual for it to stay in flower as the fruit are forming. The fruit, turquoise berries, are each backed by a green star-shaped calyx that turns bright pink and retains its color even after the fruit has dropped. I find it beautiful in flower and fascinating in fruit, but if I stopped here I wouldn't be telling the whole truth. Dr. Michael A. Dirr, a renowned authority on woody plants, writes, "In flower and fruit it is delightful but at its worst it has the appearance of an overturned Dempster Dumpster."

The sweet autumn clematis, *Clematis terniflora*, is a clematis in the midst of an identity crisis. Its name has been changed by botanists three times in the last dozen years. Formerly named *C. paniculata* and *C. maximowicziana*, at least it now has a name that is pronounceable. By whatever it is called, it is worth seeking out for its numerous frothy white flowers and sweet vanilla scent that wafts through the garden in late summer. Some growers still list and sell it under its different aliases. This rapacious vine will leap tall fences. It will also sprawl over neighboring plants and, if left undisciplined, suffocate them. After flowering, it spins silvery threads into pinwheels of fluffy seeds that float through the air to populate pretty much the entire earth. These must be pulled out in the spring wherever they sprout. But come fall, when the sweet autumn clematis whipped-cream frothed flowers bloom, all will be forgiven. After a decade I banished it from the back of the perennial garden, tired of pulling up its seedlings, but I continue to plant it on the fence bordering our property and in the woods where it can climb large trees. I love to cut long ribbons of bloom to garland a table or festoon a chandelier; it will perfume the surrounding air for a day or two without water.

Then there are the tiny honey-scented flowers of butterfly bush *(Buddleia davidii)*, heavily massed on foot-long spikes drooping off the ends of each stem. It blooms for a long time—two months or more if the dead flowers are removed. The flowers bloom in mostly soft pinks, blues, and purples, but the darker blue-black 'Black Knight' is an attention grabber. I have tried a variegated cultivar with purple flowers, but its growth is weaker and its scent less pronounced. It should be placed in a shrub border where other closely planted bushes can prop it up.

When in bloom, butterfly bushes shimmer with the iridescent colors of the butterflies that cling to them like magnets. But there can be drawbacks to their attractiveness: when I planted them alongside our tennis court they worked so well that I had trouble keeping my eye on the ball.

Chaste tree *(Vitex agnus-castus)* has a baby-powder scent that attracts butterflies, but not as well as buddleias. I have one in each of the four corners of the flower border. The two in the shade grow shorter than the two in full sun so when I cut them back in winter, I leave the shady bushes at three feet and I take the sunny ones down to a foot and a half. That way in summer they are closer in height. I always save the cut branches to use for staking lilies and making tepees for vines. I have also woven a few together for a trellis in the vegetable garden. That is how I discovered that the branches sometimes root and grow into new shrubs—the simplest way to propagate a vitex. They are easy to lift in the fall and move into a permanent place.

One fall I gave a newly sprouted chaste tree to a garden friend and the following May he sadly called to inform me that it had died. I reassured him that even in early June, they still look dead and brown, so I hide their bare branches with early-blooming large-flowered clematis. Not until mid-June do the vitex start throwing out new leaves, but once they begin, stand back: they can reach six or seven feet in two months.

One of the best-kept secrets of fall is the camelialike bloom on the Franklin tree, *Franklinia alatamaha*, named for Benjamin Franklin. A native of Georgia, it was discovered growing along the banks of the Altamaha River by John Bartram in 1770. Regrettably, it disappeared from the wild shortly after. There are references to a sighting in 1803, but the reports were doubted even at the time. So what we have are all direct descendants of Bartram's original find, reason enough to grow the Franklinia even if it weren't for its beauty and soft sweet scent. The white open-cupped flowers are punctuated with spun gold centers and continue blooming even as the leaves are changing to a blazing red. Flowers blooming among changing foliage is such an unusual sight that I would like to see the Franklin tree more widely grown.

fragrance in the winter garden All seasons, winter included, have their fragrant flowers. The Chinese witch-hazel, *Hamamelis mollis* 'Arnold Promise', has a curious yet sweet dusty exhalation,

a little like an old medicine cabinet. It is one of the most popular cultivars, because it drops its leaves, leaving its clear yellow flowers to light up the darker days of winter. The blossoms are larger than those of other cultivars, and they last longer. Each branch is decked with tousled blooms looking a little like yellow confetti left strewn about after the party is over. And it is strongly scented even on a cold day. Yet it is slow growing, so whenever I cut it I'm careful to take stock of what will be left to bloom next year. I prefer the sweeter scent of *Hamamelis mollis* 'Brevipetala', though it's not as pretty; its dried leaves cling too long, distracting attention from its tangy orange flowers. Two other equally pleasantly scented cultivars of *H.* x *intermedia* are 'Jelena', a coppery flowered variety, and 'Ruby Glow', a red.

At any other time of year, witch-hazels would deserve little more than a passing glance, but coming as they do in the dead of winter, I wholeheartedly embrace both flowers and fragrance, as a beggar does the coins in his cup. I have massed five witch-hazels to the left off the driveway for scent and winter color in a place I walk by each day. At their feet, daffodils follow their bloom. In the summer, when flowers flourish almost everywhere else on the property, the grouping of witch-hazels is a restful green. Plumbago and colchicum, both scentless but beautiful, take the place of the daffodils as underplanting to enliven the fall.

Wintersweet, *Chimonanthus praecox*, is more pleasantly scented than witch-hazel but also more temperamental. On Long Island, its bloom is easily cut short by freezing weather, and the flowers may be killed before they open. Since it blooms on last summer's growth, I'm not depleting future flowers when I cut branches for indoor cheer. Whenever it blooms without dropping too many yellow blossoms, I take it as a sign of a good garden year and count my blessings. What else is there to do? J. Barry Ferguson, a noted floral designer, calls its fragrance "an earthy and ephemeral breath, a simple smell that teases your nose. It is subtle and fleeting so you never get enough of it."

For winter, scent-seeking northern gardeners mostly need to turn their attention to fragrant indoor plants and bulbs. Two tender bulbs popular with florists are tuberoses, white tubular flowers that flare at the end and hang in pairs down the spike, and freesias, whose cupped flowers face upward lining one side of the spike. One blessing of the tuberose is that even if it is cut in tight bud all the flowers will open when put in water. Both belong to the clan of uptight flowers, rarely looking at home in a garden. I find tuberoses are easiest grown, clumped in a vegetable garden for cutting or discreetly plopped in a pot for a party where its pervasive scent (which Christopher Lloyd, the well-known English garden writer, delightfully calls "immoral") can enliven the festivities. Freesias are richly plum-scented with a firmly established reputation as a cut flower rather than a garden flower. Breeders have unfortunately gone overboard with freesias, and many of the dark red and orange cultivars are scentless. Stick with the whites, creams, and yellows—these are heavily perfumed. Ray Reddell's recommendations for sure-to-please varieties are the pale yellow 'Treasure' and the snowy 'White Swan'. Both bulbs are commonly forced for winter blooms.

Jasmine is a superstar, with its sweet-scented starry blooms, and features as an essential element in many expensive perfumes. Although many jasmines are tender, they do not pine for lack of high humidity or demand strong sun to set their spicy buds; an east or west window will suffice. Jasmine 'Maid of Orleans' has flowers that, as Tovah Martin says, "linger for several days, emitting a hauntingly spicy scent, then blush deep maroon before scattering."

The plants I've mentioned are only the most readily available and best known seductresses. As plants continue to enter commerce, there is always something new, occasionally something better. A recent discovery is *Bouvardia longiflora*, a Mexican shrub with thin white jasminelike flowers. It was promoted for the Christmas holidays as a pot plant. Scented much like a gardenia, it readily shares its fragrance.

> Women in Indonesia, India, and China traditionally scent their long hair by rolling their wet hair up around *jasmine blossoms*. If the blossoms are left in all day or overnight, the perfume of the flowers is retained in the hair for a few days.

3 the come-closers

THE FLOWERS THAT HAVE TROUBLE making their fragrance known outdoors, unless you are nearby, are those I call the come-closers. To appreciate these demure treasures fully, we must approach them closely, either by bending down—a gardener's bow to acknowledge their offering—or by gathering a few in our hand. These are more modest flowers than the seductresses; theirs is a more intimate and personal world. Unless they are planted in large groups, their scents will carry only a few feet in the garden; yet brought inside the house in bunches, their warm perfume can rise up to fill a room.

Come-closers are plentiful. Members of the group can be found in all types of plants: annuals, bulbs, perennials, shrubs, and trees.

winter into spring

BULBS

As the garden year unfolds, most of the first fragrant blooms emerge from bulbs. A mild winter will charm them into blooming earlier. These early bulbs are small and bloom close to the ground, staying low and out of the way as balmy weather capriciously alternates with torrents of sleet, snow, and rain. Gregarious creatures resplendent in bold colors, frills, and finery, they wear themselves out partying through stormy weather, then rest for the

"Some flowers spoke with strong and powerful voices, which proclaimed in accents trumpet-tongued, 'I am beautiful, and I rule.' Others murmured in tones scarcely audible, but exquisitely soft and sweet, 'I am little, and I am beloved.'"

—George Sand

remaining nine or ten months of the year. Even though the date of their first appearance varies from year to year depending on the severity of the weather, bulbs in sheltered positions always pop their heads up first. Usually it's the rash, impromptu appearance of the snowdrop's frosty bells that signal spring is on its way. At every mild opportunity they push their way up through snow and ice, sitting tight if harsh weather returns. Their sweet breath is fragile and fleeting in the cold air, yet softly released when held in a warming hand or brought indoors. I like to keep a pot of snowdrops on my desk, beside my bed, or next to my favorite chair where I can curl up and read on a snowy Sunday afternoon. Then I can make the most of their perfume. Outdoors on a cold day, a sweep of hundreds are needed to scent the air, and even then the fragrance is slight.

When the frozen ground thaws, I make a point of digging a pot of snowdrops. I prefer to take them up bulbs, roots, and all, as their stems are almost too short for cuttings and they bloom longer in pots. This also works for snow crocus, puschkinia, winter aconite, and other small bulbs, which never complain about being quickly moved indoors to continue blooming for two weeks or longer. After the abuse and flogging of winter storms, they love a mild vacation. When they have finished blooming, I return them to a different place in the garden to start a new clump for next year.

Once snowdrops lead the way, other bulbs frantically follow. Winter aconites *(Eranthis hyemalis)* are the court jesters of spring, dressed in frilled green collars to show off their shiny golden heads. I'm sure they were sent ahead to warm up the audience for the spring floral parade. These comical gnomes are full of fun and pack a powerful punch for so small a flower. Their perfume has the deep notes of a hyacinth and is easily detected when you hold one tiny flower in your hand. Sometimes they stay in bloom for almost two months. After the flowers fade and their seeds form, their frilled foliage continues to grow, remaining an attraction in the garden for many more weeks.

In the middle of this century, southern garden writer Elizabeth Lawrence wrote about receiving blooming winter aconite packed in a little soil from Mr. Krippendorf in Ohio. No matter that the mail took longer then, the bulbs survived. Today it is difficult to buy a winter aconite bulb from a supplier in the fall and have it live to bloom the following spring. By the time the bulbs reach the stores, they have spent so many months out of the ground they are often shriveled and close to death. Winter aconite lacks the protective skin surrounding most bulbs that keep them from drying out, so after purchasing them, I find it a good idea to wrap the bulbs for a few hours—or overnight—in peat moss soaked in a weak solution of liquid fertilizer. If I then can't plant them within a few hours, I place them in a plastic bag to prevent them from drying out. Once they have been plumped up this way, they must be planted within a day or two to prevent mold and rot.

A winter aconite will show gratitude for such patient and loving care. Once it comes into bloom, it is yours forever, easygoing and freely multiplying as it seeds itself about. Keep your eyes out for tiny frills of thimble-sized foliage close to the parent plant. These are the seedlings, and will be visible a year or two before they bloom.

Winter aconite is at its most beautiful as a carpet naturalized under deciduous trees or shrubs or planted into a lawn. It can be paired with such companions as blue puschkinia, snow crocus, and snowdrops, whose blooming periods will overlap. Lucky is the gardener who has a generous friend with a large planting of winter aconite, because the best time to transplant them is when they are active, even in flower.

The blooms of the snow crocus blend with the blooms of the snowdrops and the winter aconite. If planted in a protective corner, snow crocus might even bloom first, but assuredly it will mingle its sweet fragrance with the breath of the snowdrops. Holding two in your hand, it is easy to enjoy their scent. They are such small bulbs, no bigger than the top of my little finger, that they can be planted into a flower border for late winter bloom, where they will multiply freely. Even if you spade plants in and out of the border regularly, as I do, the small bulbs are rarely hurt. They roll with the punches and avoid the blows as they go forth and multiply.

Some of the other Lilliputians of spring are the dwarf iris, *Iris reticulata*, and the striped squill, *Puschkinia scilloides*. *Iris reticulata* bloom no

more than six inches above the ground with a fragrance much like that of a violet, although not as pronounced. Striped squill interest me more for their habits than their sweet scent: they emerge from the ground bloom first. If the weather isn't to their liking, they lay their yawning bells on the ground and rest, sometimes for weeks. At the first break in the weather, they again lift their heads and grow to their full height of six inches, displaying their blue-pinstriped bells on arching spikes. They can apparently be fast-frozen without damage at any stage of their growth. When the weather finally breaks, they will stick around for two months or more.

TULIPS Generally we don't think of tulips as being fragrant, but many, especially the early-blooming ones, are. Once you start looking for fragrant tulips, you'll discover a multitude. There is, for instance, *Tulipa aucheriana*, one of the smallest tulips, which produces up to three fragrant star-shaped pink flowers, each blotched with a yellow brown at its base. *T. batalinii*, *T. celsiana persica*, *T. saxatilis*, and *T. sylvestris* are also fragrant early species.

Other single early tulips planted for their sweetness of scent are 'Princess Irene', 'Alice Roosevelt', 'General de Wet', 'Bellona', 'Fred Moore', 'Lady Moore', and 'Prosperpine'. 'Princess Irene' stands out in the group because she is a flame-haired beauty sprayed with a punk rocker's purple stripe. Underneath her defiant dress is a sweet scent. She is mesmerizing—even unnerving—to behold when standing alone. My solution was to plant her in a bed of soothing ribbon grass, which calmed her jarring appearance. In other circumstances—for instance, mixed with equally colorful company—she can be visually indigestible, almost obscene.

The double early tulips 'Mr. Van der Hoef' and 'Peach Blossom' are both sweetly scented. 'Ballerina' is a fragrant lily-flowered tulip, and 'Shirley' is a single late tulip. The Darwin hybrids tend to be scentless, although there are exceptions, such as 'D Rem'. The strongest scented tulip of all, the orange parrot, 'Orange Favorite', is loved by English florists. My kids find it candy-scented, while I am reminded of ripe fruit. Because of all their frills, spring rains easily damage the parrot tulips, so as soon as they color up and before

they completely open, I cut them to bring inside. To delay their opening, they can be held for several days in the refrigerator without damage. Then in the warmth of a room, they will open.

Except for the early species, most tulips don't return reliably after the first year or two, so they should be planted where they will make a bold one-time statement—at an entrance, in a foundation planting, or in a flower border. They can also be dug after their first year and replanted in the vegetable garden, where those that do return can be cut for the house.

One of the delights of spring is to find shooting stars, *Dodecatheon meadia*, in unsuspected corners. The fact is that given their unpredictability, they are usually unsuspected. While officially not bulbs, their short spring engagement is more akin to the behavior of a bulb than a perennial. I once worried that their short bloom period might lead me to forget their location, and I'd disturb them when digging around later in the season, so I marked their places with large unattractive plant markers. I worried needlessly. Shooting stars turned out to be survivors. Still, each year, their dramatic entrance and sudden departure catch me by surprise; they never languish as the daffodils do. They can be planted between hosta or wood geranium, under sweet woodruff or ajuga in areas you won't be disturbing, and they will grow and seed themselves nearby. Shooting stars have a strong spicy odor, lilac stirred with a dash of cinnamon.

VIOLETS   What would spring be without violets? To early gardeners, the violet was the chief flower of delight and usefulness. Recipes for violet butter, violet sugar, violet oil, violet vinegar, and crystallized violets are numerous in antique herbals, gardening manuals, and cookbooks. Through the ages, violets have also seeped into beverages such as tea, lemonade, and wines. Medicinally they were used in ointments, compresses, gargles, and cosmetics. More recently, they have been featured in jams, jellies, cakes, ice cream, and numerous desserts. Besides their wonderful perfume and flavor, both the violet blossoms and leaves contain vitamin A and are exceptionally high in vita-

In seventeenth- and eighteenth-century Europe, it was a common practice to *candy flowers* to decorate cakes, puddings, and other confections. It is simple to do. Fragrant edible flowers—such as rose petals, violets, Johnny-jump-ups, and scented geraniums—work best. All you need is a gently beaten egg white, a small paintbrush, and superfine sugar. Wash the flowers gently in cool water, pat dry, paint with egg white on both sides, and sprinkle with superfine sugar. The flowers must be completely covered with egg white and sugar. Allow them to dry and harden in a colander or on a clean screen where there is good air circulation and low humidity. The egg white and sugar act a preservative, and the color and shape will last for months or even a year if stored in a cool place in a sealed container.

Caution: Don't use flowers that have been touched by poisonous chemical sprays. Many commonly grown garden flowers are poisonous—morning glories, daffodils, foxgloves—so don't experiment with flowers unless you know for sure they are safe.

min C—higher, in fact, than any domestic green vegetable. As good a reason as any to sprinkle them in salads.

In the days when they were high fashion, the correct way to sniff violets was part of the education of Victorian ladies. A deep inhalation was considered vulgar, and young ladies were taught to take a series of short, dainty sniffs when smelling the violets in their nosegays. Perhaps this was wise: violets contain ionone, a sort of odoriferous sledgehammer that when breathed deeply causes numbness. After one overenthusiastic inhalation, it may be impossible to smell anything else again until the numbness leaves a few moments later. Nevertheless, Shakespeare spoke of them only in positive terms: "Forward, not permanent, sweet, not lasting, the perfume and suppliant of a minute."

Curiously, in many of the species (the sweet violet, *V. odorata*, being one) their fragrant flowers are usually sterile, producing no seed. After the showy flowers have finished, another inconspicuous, closed, and scentless flower, known as a cleistogamous flower, forms close to the ground on a shorter stem. These are self-pollinating, and as a rule far more fruitful than the first showier flowers.

The more tender parma violets were the kind most popular for nosegays. They are doubles with a greater sweetness than the *V. odorata*. Unfortunately they are sterile, and can be propagated only by division or root cuttings. 'Marie Louise', the largest flowered and the best known parma violet, is named for Napoleon's second wife. 'Prince of Wales' came later, in 1895, and because of its longer stems was the violet most grown for the cut-flower market.

In the early decades of the twentieth century, when fashion dictated that violets be worn, close to 150 greenhouses along the Hudson River were devoted to growing them for the New York flower market. Not one exists today. Rarely are scented violets available for purchase as plants or as cut flowers. One might well ask, "Where have all the violets gone?"

In the garden, violets often bashfully hide their heads under heart-shaped leaves. The best way to enjoy them is to cut a bunch and group the flowers together in the center surrounded by a ring of heart-shaped leaves pointing outward. Tied with thin ribbons and placed in a small crystal vase, they are a romantic reminder of another era. They share their perfume and flowers for more than a week, often two. One reason they are long-lasting cut flowers is their unusual ability to absorb water through their petals. A bouquet can be submerged overnight to increase water intake and refresh the flowers.

Unfortunately, the common North American native violet is scentless, and the fragrant violets available from select catalogs and nurseries for growing in the garden are few. One of the best is *Viola odorata* 'Queen Charlotte', which blooms both in the spring and fall. There is also a strain of English violets. 'Mt. Spokane' and 'Whiskers' are two named cultivars that have large flowers, resembling pansies, and are sweetly scented.

Violets like a shady nook and do nicely in clumps along a woodland path, in a rock garden, along a stream, under the skirts of roses, or mixed with another ground cover (such as primroses) under a tree.

PRIMROSES

And we mustn't forget the primroses. *Primula* 'Mark Viette' has a loud pink flower that resembles a miniature rose and an old-rose fragrance to boot. It is long-blooming—six weeks or more. Its easy culture and agreeable nature means that it stays around in spite of neglect, and each plant increases enough to be divided into several new plants each year. In my heavy soil I've lost many a primrose but never one of these.

My favorite primrose, the cowslip primrose, *Primula veris*, is a wild-flower romping across the meadows and meandering through the woodlands of England. I love the cowslip for its sweetly scented flowers and the simple beauty of its floppy clusters of nodding yellow bells. (Occasionally, I'm told, orange or even reddish flowers are available.) The cowslip is a vigorous grower and prefers drier conditions.

Contrary to its reputation, the blossom of the common primrose, *Primula vulgaris*, has a sweet breath. It is its root that smells like licorice when the plants are lifted and divided. The common primroses are easy to grow and naturalize in meadows or woodlands.

summer into fall With the entrance of summer comes sweet alyssum, *Lobularia maritima*, hugging the earth with a glimmer of tiny white flowers. Some say it smells of new-mown hay; I think it is more honey-pot sweet. The two dogs I have had in the last fifteen years, a West Highland terrier and a golden retriever, have both been partial to napping in the alyssum. The rest of our gardens they ignore. Thank goodness alyssum seems to accept being squashed. A spray of water revives it.

While catalogs today brag of new dwarf alyssums in pink and purple, I don't relish puddles of color, and fragrance is reduced in the newer varieties, notably the pinks and purples. If you want the most scent, steer clear of the dwarf varieties. I'd prefer a mountain but have settled for a six-inch mound of alyssum, frothing like foamed milk. Also I use alyssum as a fragrant ground cover under the scentless 'Betty Prior' roses or as edging for a bed. In fact, whenever I am in doubt as to what to plant, I sow sweet alyssum. It covers a multitude of sins, weaving assorted flowers together, suppressing weeds, and scenting the ground. It readily reseeds from year to year, although often the seeds wash into the recessed edge of the garden. It is simple enough to retrieve seedlings and transplant them to where they belong. I do my own bit of yearly reseeding as early as the weather permits—about the time peas are planted. Cool weather stimulates its initial growth and it grows faster if it is not transplanted. Many books recommend shearing it back in midsummer when its bloom slows, but I have tried it and find that the sheared look is too unattractive for too long. I now do nothing and it starts to bloom again anyway.

DIANTHUS: PINKS, SWEET WILLIAM, AND CARNATIONS

Among the oldest cultivated plants are the pinks and carnations. Pinks are named for their fringed petals that look as if cut with pinking shears, not their color, although pink dominates. The six-to-eight-inch tall pinks are modest beauties that I'm sure were costumed by a mad hatter with a bag of fancy trims. Their small button flowers are tightly fringed, deeply notched, or gracefully scalloped, often with a deeper color at the heart. Their perfume is full-bodied and spicy, the forerunner of many of today's aftershave lotions. For that reason they are sometimes called clove pinks. Cottage pinks, *Dianthus plumarius*, were formerly used to flavor wine, hence their nick-name, "Sops in Wine." The China pink or annual pink, *D. chinensis*, is slightly less fragrant, but it has beautiful flowers that may be washes of a sin-gle color or freely painted—a pure white pricked with crimson and a rose color streaked with a brilliant red are two of the many choices. Even when the flowers are not in bloom, their ferny foliage, whether a silvery blue or green, is decorative.

Today pinks are sold by their cultivar name, and it is hard to tell which is hardy and which isn't. I have been pleasantly surprised to find many pinks sold to me as annuals that have stayed with me for years. It is best not to pull frostbitten plants up in the fall but to wait and see if they choose to return.

Part of the old-fashioned appeal of pinks is that they are pass-along plants. One spring I received a box of miserly pieces of assorted dianthus roots with an inch of dried stem attached. They were not much to look at and no promise of bloom could be discerned from their size. I planted them straight into the border as instructed. Coddling, I had been assured, was unnecessary. From these humble beginnings each root cutting quickly grew to flower. They now have increased to border my flower garden.

I can't explain why the English named the old-fashioned favorite *Dianthus barbatus*, Sweet William, after William, Duke of Cumberland, a bru-tal man who crushed a number of rebellions. (However, its name might explain why it was planted by the bushelful in Henry the Eighth's new garden at Hampton Court.) Certainly, a bad joke has been played on this innocent flower. The Sweet William I know proudly holds its three-inch domed cluster of small flowers two feet high, ready for picking. Each pink, red, or white flower is auricula-eyed—that is, it has a circle drawn in its middle and an outline around its edge—with contrasting white or red eye paint. Under the flowers is a fringed green beard. Sweet William is a perennial mostly grown as a biannual, normally flowering the second summer from seed. However, where growing seasons are long or when plants are started indoors ten weeks before the last frost, this species will bloom in late summer. If it is cut back after flowering, the stems thicken, making a stronger plant and prolonging its life. I planted a packet of seed one spring at the back of the vegetable garden and it has generously bloomed, reseeded, and returned freely since. Now there are so many of them—they occupy a four-foot square—that their soft sweet spicy scent reaches out to me when I am near. Generally the auricula-eyed forms have the most pronounced scent. Some of the single-color flowers are scentless. In the spring or fall, I transplant half of the clumps to the flower borders and leave the rest to use in summer bouquets and to reseed for next year's flowers.

Carnations are the showy siblings of the dianthus family and one of the three top-selling florist flowers (along with the rose and chrysanthemum). I find carnations too formal for my flower gardens, but I grow them in the cutting garden from time to time.

A new acquaintance, angelonia *(Angelonia angustifolia)*, is a tender perennial from Mexico and the West Indies that carries a light, sweet perfume with the depth and breadth of jasmine. Angelonia 'Blue Pacific' is the most remarkable. It has single white flowers with a stroke of blue paint brushed across their faces. Small as the flowers are, their unique striping is wonderfully showy when they're grown in pots or prominently displayed in a flower arrangement. In the garden they are often lost, unless you crowd them together in a large clump.

It is easy to assume that to be fragrant, flowers must be dewy and soft-petaled, but this is not true. The dry plumes of some astilbe are surpris-

ingly sweet-scented. I remember visiting a friend's garden and noticing a fragrance that I was unable to find in spite of putting my nose into many of the surrounding flowers. My hostess then calmly pointed to a patch of 'Peach Blossom' astilbe surrounding the base of a tree. The feathery peach plumbs had been right in front of me the whole time, yet I had never thought to smell them. This taught me a lesson.

Each spring I grow two American native lupines from seed: *Lupinus perennis*, a perennial wildflower, which sends up three-foot spikes lined with blue pealike blooms, each with a soft honeylike scent; and the annual lupine better known as the Texas bluebonnet, which blooms closer to the ground, six to sixteen inches, with a lively, more intense sweetness. I start a row of perennial lupines each summer in the well-drained raised bed of the cutting garden to move into the formal garden the following spring. In the heavy clay soil of the formal garden I lose a few older ones each winter. It's really not much trouble, as they are easy to grow from seed. A local told me when I moved here that all perennial lupines were treated as annuals because of the soil, so I take great pride in my survivors.

It isn't necessary to live in Texas to enjoy the bluebonnets. They grow as an ornamental anywhere the season is long enough, blooming in fall in New York instead of in spring as they do in Texas. I have grown them in my cutting garden and even seeded them in a corner of our driveway where the drainage is excellent.

Daylilies are another family generally not thought to be fragrant, but there are choice daylily cultivars that blare sweet scents from their large trumpets—not a huge number, it is true, but enough to be worth searching out. The fragrant ones, such as 'Chicago Comanche', are softly sweet-scented, and each has a scent different from the next. They tend to be such yellow varieties as 'Mayan Gold', 'Resurrection Yellow', 'Lemon Cap', 'Fragrant Light', 'Ida Miles', and 'Hyperion' (as well as its cousins, 'Hyperion Elite' and 'Hyperion Supreme'), but fragrant daylilies can be found in the full range of colors. 'Hosanna' is a combination of golden orange and melon, 'Ming Snow' is a creamy apricot, 'Pink Tangerine' looks like its name, 'Root

Beer' has dark cherry-red blooms, 'Scarlet Apache' is just that, and you can guess the color of 'Rooten Tooten Red'.

There are other wildflowers and woodland plants that whisper sweetly. The yellow lupine, *Thermopsis caroliniana*, has blue-green leaves and a light sweet fragrance and brightens a partially shaded spot. The flat purple flower heads of Joe Pye weed *(Eupatorium purpureum)* are a mass of smaller flowers packed together to make a big impression—from twelve to eighteen inches across. Its vanilla scent, coming at summer's end, is welcome in my garden. The flower's origins as a roadside weed growing up to seven feet tall don't deter me, since its hybrids are shorter and well-behaved. Actually, the taller plants are architectural building blocks in British gardens.

Blue lace flower, *Trachymene coerulea*, is another I grow only in the cutting garden for fall bouquets, mostly because it takes more than three months to bloom from seed. If I started it indoors (and next year I might), it would be lovely in any border. It is a lacy, soft blue beauty (imagine a blue Queen Anne's lace) with a sweet baby-powder scent. I recently purchased a bunch at a California farm stand to take to my uncle on a hospital visit. In the elevator going up to his floor, several passengers admired their scent and asked me the name. Since most people hate to start conversations with strangers in elevators, that may say something about just how charming blue lace flower can be.

4 moonlighters

MY FAVORITE TIME in the garden is the hour or two just before sunset, when the contrast between light and dark is muted and shadows lengthen. The low-slung shafts of light cast a golden net catching the tallest flowers, and they shimmer as if gilded. Pigment stolen at noon by the scorching sun is lavishly returned at dusk. It is then that each flower wears its most glowing colors.

The garden's beauty is irresistible in early evening. This is a time to pause, a time to rejoice, a time to reflect and quietly observe the sun's dramatic bow as it exits. It is also a time of explosive scent as the timid flowers that hide their fragrance until late afternoon embrace the evening by releasing perfumed currents into the garden. The intensity of their scent compensates for the waning light. These are the plants I call moonlighters, and at dusk they join those day-scented flowers that continue to distill their perfume into the night. As the sun sets, more often than not the breeze is hushed, seemingly out of reverence for the flowers. A garden in moonlight is a perfumer's paradise.

A moonlit garden is designed to be at its best after hours, to extend the day for the weary and enhance the pleasure of relaxed dining outdoors in the quiet evening. So all the plants I have included here are summer bloomers, to draw the gardener out on a warm night. The tradition reaches back to countries of high heat, such as Persia and India, where a garden could only be enjoyed after sunset, when the heat of the day had passed. They were the original moonlight gardens.

"It is a curious fact that many sweet scented flowers withhold their fragrance during the day and pour it out to the night. And it is these vespertine flowers, as someone has called them, that we chiefly enjoy at night, for there is a special poignancy in their sweetness not to be found in the simpler perfumes of the daytime hours."
—LOUISE BEEBE WILDER,
The Fragrant Path

61

Moonlight doesn't recognize colors. The garden greens recede to black, and the whites, blushing pinks, and pale yellows emerge. But only the contours of lightly colored flowers can be discerned, their shapes flawlessly traced against a shadowed background. Color is not necessary in evening-scented flowers and might even be unwanted, making the flowers invisible when they need to shine in the dark. Fortunately, night-scented flowers are often white, and can play tricks with your imagination. Some of the larger flowers float on the breeze like garden ghosts. The white, softly bending, starry flowers of the peacock orchid *(Gladiolus callianthus,* formerly *Acidanthera murieliae)* have dark centers that disappear with the waning light, making them look like great butterflies swaying over the garden. They are as easily grown as the more common gladiolus, needing the same cultural care. Yet when I dig up the tender corms in the fall to store away from frost for the winter, I find many more baby corms or cormels around the peacock orchid. These can be grown on the following summer among the vegetables and placed into the border the year after when they are mature enough to flower. They are one of the most reasonably priced bulbs, perhaps because they increase so readily. I don't understand why they aren't grown more.

If at all possible, plant night-scented flowers with a western exposure to catch the last rays of the sun. The additional warmth will increase the amount of perfume they spill into the night air to attract their pollinators, the moths, beetles, and butterflies.

Though few of us see it, there is a wonderful theatrical performance by pollinators after dark. Moths, for example, are usually nocturnal, and many night-blooming flowers are designed with trumpet-shaped or tubular blooms accessible only to the moth's long tongues. In their search for nectar, the fluttering of white-winged species adds a sparkle to the bolder flower shapes as they pollinate such plants as crinum and honeysuckle. Fragrance is stronger in blossoms pollinated by beetles, particularly flowers that emit a "fruity" perfume, such as some tree peonies.

A moonlight garden needn't exclude flowers that are not white, but it is the white flowers that give the garden its beauty. A clump of completely

white flowers, either of the same variety or mixed, hold and reflect the light, creating a faintly gleaming beacon. The larger the flowers and the flatter the surface, the more light they catch and reflect.

The plants I grow for their beauty and scent in the moonlight are all strongly night-scented and mostly white. They all begin as summer bloomers, and many stay into the fall. Summer is the season I spend most evenings in the garden. It becomes our outdoor dinning room.

annuals Annuals dominate my nighttime plantings, and they are all easy to grow if you know their peculiarities. Angel's trumpet, *Datura metel*, and the moonflower, *Ipomoea alba*, are my favorites, even though each blossom opens only for one night, fading when morning comes. By then they have completed their night's work of attracting moths for pollination. However, these energetic annuals stretch, bud, and bloom nonstop for many months. Their flowers can be picked and brought inside for an evening's enjoyment. The flowers of datura, if picked just as they open and before they have been pollinated, last two or three days in water—hoping, I suppose, to attract a night-flying visitor.

On my white angel's trumpet, *Datura metel* 'Alba', a soft, velvety green pouch covers each bud. As the flower grows, so does the pouch, until it finally splits open and the lime green, accordion-pleated skirt of the flower emerges in late afternoon of one day, then the flower bleaches white and opens the following evening. From dusk to dawn, its white trumpets boldly blare out its almost too sweet and musty scent, which echoes that of paper-white daffodils. It is best to let the scent drift to you rather than put your nose into the petals; a close whiff ends in an off-note. Since a datura blossom is a one-night stand, the trumpets close and begin to collapse around noon the next day. A few days later, petals fall, and a spiky seedpod, resembling the spiked balls twirled by gladiators, begins to develop, its threatening appearance reminding the gardener to beware: all parts of a datura are poisonous and can be deadly.

With their poisonous character, the various daturas have a colorful history. In India, thugs employed preparations of the plant to stupefy their victims, and South American Indians dazed wives and slaves with datura potions for burial alive to accompany their dead masters into the hereafter. The jimsonweed *(Datura stramonium)*, a native of the tropics naturalized in North America, has caused trouble for men and animals alike. British soldiers sent in the early spring of 1676 to quell a rebellion in Jamestown, Virginia, cooked and ate young jimsonweed sprouts. They became insane for a period of eleven days before recovering. While not a plant to ingest, datura is no more dangerous to grow than the foxgloves, oleander, morning glories, daffodils, and other poisonous plants that frequent our gardens. Small children, of course, should be warned about all of them.

The spiky datura's seedpod starts out small and continues to grow until it is the size of a plum. Inside the spiked ball, seeds are arranged in a white pulp as in a tomato. When the seeds are ripe, the ball splits to spill and spread its seeds—I counted 213 in one pod. The flat, tan seeds are small yet easy to plant individually. There is no need to deadhead your datura, incidentally; the blooms continue and even increase at the same time as the plant is setting seed. Each spring numerous datura seedlings sprout around our pool. I originally planted them there to add light and scent to an evening swim. There are always so many little ones that I pot up several for friends, moving others to containers on the terrace where we sit in the evenings. Since they are so big at maturity—four feet high and nearly as wide—I leave only a few to grow at poolside. The plant growing in partial sun (full morning sun, the shade of a large umbrella in the afternoon), grew to the largest size, and flowered several weeks sooner than those grown in full sun or full shade. But daturas accommodate themselves readily to a range of conditions. One drawback must be mentioned. So far as scent is concerned, daturas have dual personalities (see page 99)—while the flowers smell good, the leaves have the fusty odor of an attic boarded up for years. Still, if you don't bruise a leaf, its bad body odor will remain secret.

MOONFLOWERS

Moonflowers are an obvious choice for a nighttime planting: they light up the garden at dusk and on cloudy days with large, round, intensely fragrant flowers. The blossoms open early in the evening and close before noon the next day. However, if the day is overcast and dark, they are fooled into opening earlier or staying open later. Their heart-shaped leaves are large, often reaching up to eight inches, and their stems can be prickly, as they are covered with fine hairs, so handle the vine carefully. Moonflower's heavenly scent is concentrated in the oil between the central bands inside each open flower. While each flower lasts but one night, there are many more waiting in the wings, and the buds come fast and furious till frost. It is as though they are speeding up and flowering even more lavishly on each successive night.

Unfortunately, I have found moonflowers to be temperamental. The first few times I grew them there was nothing to it, and they bloomed easily from early August long into fall, even after the first frosts. Now it seems I can't do anything right. Having captured my heart with its round bride-white face and heavy exotic perfume, it plays hard to get. Sometimes the vine grows to blooming size and sometimes it doesn't; I can never understand its reasons. Being greedy for flowers around the clock, I have fallen back on growing moonflowers and morning glories together.

The first potential stumbling block when growing moonflowers is their hard seed shell, which makes it difficult for the plant embryo to break through. To speed germination, soak the seeds in water at room temperature several hours before planting, or leave them overnight rolled in a moist paper towel in order to soften the outer shell. A quicker method is to score the outer shell with a file to allow the embryo to break through. Better yet, do both. Higher germination will result.

Take care in setting out young moonflowers in the garden. I have lost many by not waiting long enough after the last frost date. They need warm nights and a less abrupt exposure to changing temperatures than most annuals. Harden them off by putting them outside during the day and indoors at night for four or five days before leaving them outside all night. If the night temperature falls into the forties during their first two weeks outdoors, either bring them inside or cover them with a garden blanket or newspaper. By fall, they take low temperatures in their stride and continue blooming even on frosty nights.

Sown directly outside, the seeds won't grow until both the soil and air are warm, so nothing is gained by planting them too early, and the seeds will rot if the soil is too wet and cold. Once the plants begin to grow, protect them from strong winds and give them a trellis, string, or a fence to clamber on. They climb by twining around a support, completing a circle in three hours. They flower more if they are not fertilized, so save the fertilizer. I usually start the seeds indoors six to eight weeks before they are to be planted outdoors. According to Burpee bloom charts, moonflowers are supposed to bloom approximately ninety to a hundred days after sowing, but I've had blooms on small vines confined in pots at sixty days and been kept waiting for blooms to appear on vines planted into the garden at a hundred and twenty days. So although moonflowers are contrary, try them anyway: they are full of possibilities and their perfume will entrap you. They make a wonderful backdrop to a garden when grown on a fence; they can also be planted to climb up to a second-story deck or to wreath a dining-room window. They are fine on a terrace—I planted one in a three-gallon pot and it more than covered a tepee of five-foot bamboo poles. Once the vines take off, they climb to the top of the tepee and then start back down, cascading over themselves without seeming to mind. I have also grown them in oversized terrace pots mixed with upright flowers. They draped over the sides of the pots and glided onto the terrace like a bridal train.

PETUNIAS

Petunias, another old-fashioned annual, have changed greatly through the decades as breeders, growers, and gardeners have worked with them. Scented petunias are among the sweetest smelling flowers, especially the old single white, light mauve, and dark blue varieties. The blues in general are the strongest scented. Louise Beebe Wilder wrote, "The scent of petunia is not altogether pleasant save at night when it loses a certain coarseness of quality and becomes lighter and more transparent." I don't know about that; I do know I notice their sweet scent more in the late afternoon and evening. If you are looking for fragrance, take care—there are many scentless new introductions in all colors. The only sure way to buy a scented petunia is to smell the flower first. Even though it is not in the best interest of the petunia (or any other annual) to bloom in its six-pack, growers know customers will buy more if a flower is present, and that is the way they are most often sold. A prudent gardener, however, practices "tough love" by removing any flowers when planting a blooming petunia into the garden, thus forcing the plant to concentrate on developing roots. The result is longer bloom, less stress, and more flowers through its lifetime.

I don't plant petunias into the garden. They sprawl too much for my taste. Yet petunias sprawling over the sides of window boxes strike me as heavenly, especially the ones hanging under my bedroom window. I also use them in pots at the entrance and on the terrace. Their lush growth and sprawling habit has them trailing on the ground by autumn.

Two annuals whose common names place them perfectly are evening stock and night-scented stock. Evening stock *(Matthiola longipetala)*, with its small petals in disarray, looks like an unkempt, long-limbed schoolgirl needing her hair combed. I made the mistake of seeding them for cutting in the vegetable garden, a place I rarely frequent at night, so I barely made their acquaintance. Next time I'll plant them where I'll enjoy them on warm summer nights. I have to say that in my limited experience thus far, the scent of evening stock is nothing to get excited about—lovely but subtle—although that might have been the fault of the variety I grew.

The night-scented stock *(Matthiola bicornis)* is only twelve inches high, with wispy white flowers that appear to be lightly washed with grape juice. It is intensely sweet, and the fragrance carries a fair distance on the evening breeze. Its toughness belies its frail appearance and, as the sun goes down, its scent increases, being strongest after dark. Wayne Winterrowd describes its fragrance as "a raspberry tart with an almond crust." All stocks are best planted in a pot that can be carried into the house in the evening or planted under an open window. It is less important that they be seen; but make sure they are in a place where their fragrance can be enjoyed.

Some of the nicotiana family's tallest members are also strongly scented, especially at night. *Nicotiana sylvestris*—woodland tobacco or candelabra tobacco—has a scent reminiscent of freesias. It is a lovely sight at the back of a garden when it reaches its full five-foot height and holds its white thin tubular flowers aloft, clustered like a softly lit candelabrum. *Nicotiana alata* has narrow trumpet-shaped flowers loosely dangling from its stems. It is commonly called the jasmine tobacco, after its scent. Its shorter, three-foot height places it in the middle of the border. Five or seven of these large plants grouped together catch the moonlight. The most commonly grown foot-high nicotianas, 'Nicki Hybrids', are scentless. Why their popularity surpasses that of their scented siblings confounds me. I suspect it has to do with the fact that seed companies make more money on hybrids than on species.

South America is the birthplace of the four-o'clock, a colorful annual in neon pinks, yellows, and white. Four-o'clocks open before four in the afternoon, earlier if planted in the shade. Their perfume is unmistakably scented of orange blossoms. This is an annual that takes you back to grandma's garden, if you were lucky enough to have had a grandma who gardened. In her day, four-o'clocks were as popular as impatiens—scentless, alas—are today. They are easy to grow from seed, and their two-foot height places them in the edging of a garden or as a frill at the base of a shrub. They can also be grown in a pot or as a houseplant to take indoors when frost is expected. They will bloom indoors if temperatures are kept close to 65 degrees.

The dame's rocket, *Hesperis matronalis*, is a three-foot-tall wildflower that readily reseeds. Its perfume is a mix of violets and damask roses. As is usually the case, the double form is stronger scented. I can understand why Hungarian ladies grew dame's rocket in pots outdoors and then moved them indoors to scent their bedrooms at night. I must try it.

An easygoing wildflower, dame's rocket accepts sun or partial shade, appearing suddenly in the spring, blooming for two months, and then slip-

ping quietly into oblivion. I rarely see it growing today, although it also makes a good long-lasting cut flower. Unlike many old-fashioned flowers, the seed is not hard to obtain. While I wouldn't grow it in a flower border because it leaves a hole when it departs in summer, I have sprinkled it on a bank where it basks in the sun, along a woodland path, and in a wildflower meadow. If you add it to a flower border, it can be pulled out and replaced with an annual after it flowers; all you need to leave is a plant or two from which to collect seed for next year's flowers. Dame's rocket is a biannual and is best seeded immediately after collection.

perennials
Perennials are the staples of most flower gardens, and a moonlight garden is no exception. The gas plant, *Dictamnus albus*, is a perennial that fascinates me as much for its strangeness as for its perfume. Its white or rose-colored flowers perch along the top of a three- to four-foot stem. From here their scent can take flight—a scent suggestive of a blend of anise, sweet clover, and lavender. (One writer detects a strong hint of turpentine when smelled up close.) The scent is noticeable at some distance on a warm and humid evening. If the night is still and the plant has recently opened, it gives off a volatile oil. Hold a match above a blossom and the gas will ignite with a tiny puff of flame that will hurt neither you nor the flower.

Unhappily, today the gas plant is out of favor, mostly forgotten after being cherished and cultivated for over four hundred years. One explanation might be that it can take three to four years before a plant comes into flower, and it is costly for commercial growers to wait that long. Even gardeners, who should know better, are too impatient for quick results. Over time, gas plants form large clumps and have an average lifetime longer than you or I, and the wait is worth it. I regard them as the old reliables in the flower border.

VINES
Vines are the least utilized fragrant plants, yet they make the greatest difference in a garden, adding spread and height as they carry their scent up and

shower it back down. The flowers of the Japanese honeysuckle (*Lonicera japonica halliana*) sit on their stems in pairs and hang in long tresses. Upon opening at dusk, they are pure white and strongly scented of honeysuckle, yet with the depth and sweetness of a gardenia, a complex perfume attracting night-flying moths. After fertilization, the corollas turn pale yellow. If as a child you ever plucked a white blossom of honeysuckle and sucked the drop of nectar out, you know why "nectar" is a synonym for intense sweetness. If you haven't, it's not too late to try.

It is this same Japanese honeysuckle that rivals kudzu as a scourge in the South. But though it can get out of hand, it is really worth growing—and controlling—for its wonderful fragrance. A vine of it wreaths my front door; I was told by the previous owner that it has been growing there for eighty-five years. I have not had a problem with its crowding out other plants or seeding itself around the garden, although its verdant sprawl over the trellis at the front door makes visitors wonder if I'm familiar with the concept of pruning. My response is simple: If they came home after dark to be greeted by its scent or were cheered on rainy days by its far-reaching perfume, they would not do much pruning either. Better yet, if they arose invigorated each warm summer morning when its perfume floats into the bedroom as they awakened, they might doubt that I could ever bring myself to prune it at all. But living in a house entirely smothered in honeysuckle could be dangerous—I would be too joyful to ever leave. When I do go out for the day, I frequently nip a fragrant blossom to carry along. Today there are many honeysuckles on the market that have no fragrance, so check before you purchase.

The chocolate vine, *Akebia quinata*, known for its rampant growth, is night-scented and spring-flowering. I only know of its stronger scent at night because one spring evening I visited a friend and her front porch pillars were twined with akebia. Jack-in-the-Beanstalk would have reached the clouds sooner (I'm exaggerating just a little) if he had planted akebia instead of his beanstalk—it will grow fifteen or more feet the first year. But with little regular care and a hatchet, you can have a gracefully twining, woody vine to train on a fence or a wall or over a porch. Scarcely showy, the akebia's five-fingered foliage is delicate and visually softens hard surfaces. Its spicy vanilla-scented flowers are muddy maroon, and many hide under spring's new leaves. These are the female flowers and are about an inch across. The small clusters of male flowers are a rosy purple, half an inch across. In the fall, purple-violet, sausagelike pods up to four inches long appear. If you prune an akebia with care, you'll be able to see the flowers more easily, because the vine isn't wrapping around itself. And the scent is available to be enjoyed even when the flowers are hidden. I have akebia decorating a grape arbor where I can cut long strands for swags at a dinner party, sometimes draping it over a chandelier. The foliage will stay fresh out of water for as long as a day. Shorter lengths are perfect for filling out a flower arrangement.

The golden trumpet vine, *Allamand cathartica* 'Williamsii', has a sweet fruity fragrance, especially at night—it has whimsically been described as "wine after dark." This is a tender vine for those of us who garden in the North. Grow it in a pot with decorative treillage for it to climb. It has no difficulty living eight months of the year as a houseplant if it gets good light.

QUEEN OF THE NIGHT

There are many fragrant houseplants to grow that will light up the night indoors, so don't despair if you don't have a garden. One of the most peculiar characters is the Queen of the night *(Epiphyllum oxypetalum)*, also commonly called night-blooming cereus, although it does not belong to the cereus family. When flower-clothed it is a most glorious sight: each fragrant flower is luminous and lovely, glistening white in the darkness, sweetly scenting the room with an exotic perfume with the depth, trail, and carry of paperwhites. But bloom is very short indeed—only one night a year. Naked the other 364 nights and all the days of the year, Queen of the night is so homely only a mother could love it, lanky and long, all arms and legs. Its flattened leaflike stems are made of jointed segments and mostly sprawl and flop awkwardly in all directions. On my plant, one stem stands straight up, branching at the top into what might be described as the flattened fingers of a hand. How it holds this pose outdoors in the summer garden, through rain and wind without support, is a mystery. Of course, I could lop it off. This wouldn't improve its appearance much, but I could send the chopped-off segments to a gardening friend for propagation, which is how I got my own Queen; it is a plant to be shared.

When I first received small jointed sections of a stem, I let them air-dry for a few days before sticking them all into a single pot. I hadn't expected the lot to root, and in my ignorance I simply left them there to grow crowded together. As luck would have it, the Queen of the night prefers being root-bound. Only when you see roots actually growing out the bottom of the pot is it time to move her into a bigger container.

It was several years before my plants bloomed, and when they did, I missed the show. All I caught was the morning after, when the flowers were hanging their heads. The next year, determined to see it bloom, I moved the plant to the center of the kitchen table as soon as the buds set and cleared my calendar. Each day the buds puffed up like slow-filling balloons until they were three inches fat and six inches long. (On a mature plant they would be bigger still—nine inches by six.)

Finally, as nine o'clock approached one evening, the buds began opening a layer at a time, petticoats and flounces of petals emerging to surround the mouth of the flower. Inside each flower was the best show: an intricate pattern composed of dozens of stamens, capped with gold buttons, stood and saluted. Prominently shining in the middle was a stigma opening as a starburst. The blossoms sported twelve to fourteen rays.

As a houseplant, Queen of the night has simple needs, living a long and happy life in filtered light on a sunny windowsill. Water it when dry and fertilize it monthly in the spring and summer. Its cultural needs are little different from those of its near relation the Christmas cactus.

A final gothic note about the night-blooming cereus: in the tropics of Central and South America where the plant is at home, its large blossoms are pollinated by bats. As the garden writer Tovah Martin has observed, this makes it "the perfect plant for your belfry."

■   ■   ■

In planning and planting a moonlight garden, pay particular attention to the areas you frequent at night. Maybe it's the entrance to the back door, a front porch with rocking chairs, or a terrace where you like to dine out. Next, ask yourself which months you frequent the area most. If you regularly vacation away from home in July, concentrate on flowers that bloom in June, August, and September. To make the most of your moonlighters, include many day-scented flowers as well.

A true moonlit garden should be designed with pockets of white flowers or composed entirely of white flowers. An all-white garden is a beautiful sight and something I have envied. But it is tough to plant. I have tried several times. Once I started with all-white flowers along the driveway to light up the night. The next thing I knew I couldn't resist adding blue monkshood for fall color. Then pink astilbe crept in, and you can guess the rest. But perhaps you are more disciplined than I am, and can avoid falling in love with every flower you meet. It's an enterprise worth attempting.

5 | the shaggy dogs

THE AROMATIC PLANTS are shaggy dogs—their scent is tightly guarded, hidden in their foliage rather than in their flowers. They beg to be petted, for it is when their foliage is stroked, scratched, or crushed (rather like a "scratch and sniff" perfume ad) that their fragrance is released.

If heavy sweet perfumes are not to your liking, the earthy smell of these aromatics might become your favorites. Some are sweet, some bitter, some pungent, and some astringent, but nearly all are refreshing, cleansing, and stimulating.

An aromatic plant holds its essential oil in tiny cells either on the surface of its leaves or deeply embedded within them. Scented geraniums and thyme hold their oils in cells on the surface, yielding them readily when lightly stroked or touched by a soft rain or a strong ray of sunshine. Amazingly, no matter where or how many times the leaves are stroked, they never seem to use up their essential oils. Sweet bay *(Laurus nobilis)* and pineapple sage are two plants whose leaves must be scratched, crushed, or broken before the aroma is released.

Generally, leaves hold their perfume longer than blossoms, and when dried they are stronger scented than when fresh. In dried leaves, essential oils become more concentrated. This is the reason cooks need to use a larger quantity of a fresh herb in a recipe than they do of the same herb dry.

Most herbs are aromatic plants, but there are many other aromatics besides herbs. Broken leaves of tomato plants release a tangy tomato aroma even when no fruit is present.

"As for the garden of mint, the very smell of it alone recovers and refreshes our spirits, as the taste stirs up our appetite for meat."

—PLINY THE ELDER

75

Many grasses, when cut, freshen the air with their scent, and a number of the plants with sweetly fragrant flowers also have an odor locked in their leaves. Sometimes it's the same sweet scent as in the flower or, on occasion, it is different (but usually pleasant). So when pruning or removing dying foliage, don't be surprised if you're greeted by a scent where you might not expect to find one. The real stinkers in this category are discussed in detail in the dual-personality section (see page 99).

Since shaggy dogs nap in the garden, growing fat with the promise of scent until rudely awakened, they should be grown in a position where they are likely to be brushed against, trod on, or plucked. For example, to enjoy their fragrance in the garden, tough aromatic creepers are best suited to be grown on a path or between stones or bricks on a terrace where they will be stepped on. The taller, more delicate plants can be placed where a passerby will brush against them on a walk through the garden or in a meadow. Of course, the alternative is to enjoy their fragrance only when you stop to pet them, pick them, or move them indoors. Take advantage of beautiful foliage by planting them wherever they look good. Then they can be cut for floral arrangements, hung dried for winter arrangements, steeped for tea, chopped for cooking, or used to scent potpourri.

There is no point in organizing the shaggy dogs by their season of bloom, since it is their foliage fragrance we value. Evergreen plants such as balsam and thyme can provide year-round scent outside, while tender perennials grown as houseplants, such as scented geraniums and rosemary, will delight us indoors in every season.

It may be helpful to suggest particular places these plants can be grown to get the most from their fragrance. But remember that many of them prefer the barren soil and dry Mediterranean conditions they are accustomed to at home. Even though I was aware of this twenty years ago when I designed

a circular herb garden at the entrance to my vegetable and cutting-flower garden, I couldn't help myself. Like an eager young mother overfeeding her children, I made a raised bed with enriched soil. Restraint is the hardest thing to learn in gardening. In those early years, the lavender languished, the santolina died, the mint was triumphant, and the roses were glorious. I put this down to the simple fact you can't please all the people all the time. But I should have been tipped off by the discovery that those herbs that did flourish were not very flavorful. Rich soil diluted their essential oils.

Mother Nature in all her wisdom showed me the way. I find that the more I pay attention to what the plants are actually doing in the garden, the better the garden becomes and the easier it is to care for. On another occasion, the herbs simply moved on to a place that they preferred to the one I offered them.

When we expanded an area of the driveway to allow for more parking, we built a three-foot-high stone retaining wall. On top of the wall and between the stones, I installed small plants and creepers, best viewed up close. Many were selected for their delicate features and sweet breaths, which we wanted to smell without stooping to the ground.

It was not a rock garden in the classic sense, although many traditional rock-garden plants have found their way there. Over the years, a smattering of plants on top of the wall seeded themselves in the gravel driveway—the one place on the property with quick drainage. Under the gravel is a gritty soil with few nutrients. I liked the way it looked and took it a step further, envisioning a mirror garden reflecting the pattern of plants on the top of the wall at its base, as if they had spilled over or flung themselves down. I still couldn't believe that the plants were happy in this wretched soil. So I removed the gravel three feet out from the wall, dug down six inches and enriched the grit with compost and topsoil before planting an assortment of herbs and flowers and replacing an inch of gravel on top of the soil to act as a mulch and to blend in with the rest of the driveway.

In less than a year my vision became a reality, but Mother Nature again took me by surprise. The unimproved part of the driveway has sprouted more than the improved part. Fragrant plants and aromatics such as pansies, violets, bigroot geranium *(Geranium macrorrhizum)*, assorted thyme, nepeta, and thimble-sized spots of golden feverfew *(Chrysanthemum parthenium* 'Aureum') seeded themselves and thrived. They dotted the gravel up to eight feet from the wall. Of course, many of these plants grow well enough in other soils, but I've never grown them with so strong a scent or had them so readily reseed. This is where I now successfully grow assorted lavender and santolina, the two aromatic herbs that I previously overindulged to the point of an early death. In the gravel garden Spanish lavender *(Lavandula stoechas)* and the English lavender, *Lavandula angustifolia* 'Hidcote', along with other sundry and assorted lavenders, grow luxuriantly. Lavender cotton *(Santolina chamaecyparissus)*, a strongly pungent aromatic shrub, doubled its girth in a year. 'Lemon Queen', a dwarf gray foliage cultivar with a slightly sweet pungency that I am fond of, is also at home here.

The corner of the driveway where cars used to be parked has now become so floriferous that in some cases cars must be parked on the lawn. It has occasionally happened that an insensitive driver has parked in my gravel garden, so my latest addition is a foot-high stone wall curving to mirror the shape of the retaining wall and about six feet out from it. This makes my gravel garden official, and flatly states "No Trespassing."

designing with aromatics— herbs in particular

Aromatics are valued for their foliage, rarely for their flowers. Visually, the foliage of aromatics often adds texture, color, and substance to a planting. If the foliage lasts throughout the garden season, it can be used to complement and contrast with fragrant flowers and shrubs. And what a great selection there is, from the golden feverfew, silvery lavender, and purple perila to the assorted greens, dappled and streaked with cream, that belong to the scented geranium's extended

family. Yet because most aromatics have been stereotyped as herbs, they are often excluded from the very best places, such as rose gardens, flower beds, and shrub borders. This is a pity, and not only because of their attractiveness. By integrating them with other plants, I am probably furnishing some preventive medicine. Any aromatic foliage that doesn't attract chewing insects may actually help repel pests.

I don't indiscriminately mix herbs into all of my gardens. My first criteria in the flower beds are sweet scent and beautiful blooms. But contrasting foliage colors such as herbs provide may help draw attention to the flowers. Silver, gold, and light green backlight my favorite flowers. The sharper contrast of dark foliage—purple, burgundy, and dark green—set their floral partners in sharp relief and make them seem closer.

Roses grown with bare or even mulched soil tend to get muddy skirts. An herbal ground cover can stop this and can also serve as a protective barrier to keep soil-borne bacteria from attacking the rose foliage. I make no claims that this is a scientific fact; I only know that my roses have had fewer diseases and problems since I surrounded them with herbs. As I mentioned in a previous chapter, I've underplanted my formal rose garden with nepeta, society garlic *(Tulbaghia violacea variegata)*, globe allium, and lavender as much for their beauty as for their fragrance. The climbing and shrub roses planted to decorate and disguise the tennis court are underplanted with lamb's ear. Its silvery leaves have the softness of cashmere and a sweetly pungent scent when rubbed.

The gravel garden is gilded with golden feverfew as it travels around the base of the rock wall and adds golden sunlight and sparkle amid the gravel mulch. Silver gleams from the lamb's ear, lavender, santolina, and variegated thyme.

Tansy, with its exquisitely cut light green leaves and long-blooming clusters of yellow buttons, jogs around the meadow under our fruit trees, adding a pleasant contrast to the unkempt grasses. From midsummer to frost I can cut the flowers for winter's dried arrangements. In the meadow I also let

loose comfrey *(Symphytum officinale)*, with its oversized load of velvety gray-green leaves and tiny blue flowers. Here they can both romp together without getting into mischief, and as I walk among them and brush their leaves, I can enjoy their pungent breaths. The lawn mower cuts them off at their knees several times a summer, and that keeps them in check.

Parsley adds a ruffle to the edge of my cottage garden. (Its essential oil holds the pleasant memory of my grandmother's cooking. I see her sitting on her stool and stirring parsley into a soup pot or picking and eating it raw as "the world's best breath refresher.") Lemon verbena *(Melissa officinalis)* roams the woods with its crinkled light green leaves. (It must have been planted as a seedling hitchhiking on another plant.) Its lemony scent is wonderful when a leaf is rubbed, so I don't mind the job of weeding it out as much as dealing with other rambling fellows.

Purple perilla, or the beefsteak plant *(Perilla frutescens)*, with its dark burgundy leaves washed with an iridescent light purple, hops on four-foot stilts throughout the formal flower bed. I often leave it when it lands behind a pink, blue, or purple flower. It is a relative of basil and adds a similar tang with a pinch of cinnamon to the air when you brush against it.

Mints are as famous for their scents as for their rambling ways. A variegated mint runs along the stream near the back door, and I pick it occasionally for summer's cool drinks. I still regret having planted assorted mints twenty years ago, because they are almost uncontrollable. Every spring I'm still weeding out a few stragglers. There are herbs that shouldn't be turned loose anywhere, and mints are the prime example. My mints are now planted in solitary confinement, each variety in its own cell.

Of course, I have a separate garden devoted to a mix of ornamental and culinary herbs. I can't break completely away from traditional gardening, as much as I admire those who do. It is planned and planted each spring as a combination of textures and foliage colors. It always looks a little bare in May and June, waiting for the annual herbs to fill out. But by July it fills in and it continues to increase in beauty throughout the summer and long into the fall.

scented walks and scented terraces

When bathing was infrequent, cut herbs such as lavender and wormwood were strewn on the floors of churches and houses to disguise body odors. While herbs are no longer used this way, many of them are rugged enough to be walked on and can be planted in cracks in paths or between stepping-stones. Even the smallest shaggy dogs that don't look like much in a garden may have the beauty and scent to transform a nondescript walk into a pleasurable stroll. Add miniature bulbs to the herbs and an ordinary, functional stone path set simply in a lawn may become a garden feature. Used this way, many a homely herb may turn heads and make people smile because of its pleasing personality. A quick dash from here to there becomes an extraordinary journey of discovery, offering a chance to marvel at the aroma and beauty of some of the garden's smallest creepers.

The best plants for growing between stepping-stones are the tough ones with textured leaves that sprawl, laying their heads on the stone, across a path or skirting a terrace, such as thyme, pennyroyal, and German chamomile. When walked on, they instantly release their aromas, which rise to surprise the stroller pleasantly. On the hottest days, they are nature's smelling salts.

Take thyme, for example. Traditionally, the smell of thyme was thought to raise the spirits. Why not accept the truth of this and line a path with thyme to cheer guests as they arrive at your door? It will send waves of a pungent, cleansing fragrance into the air when stepped on. An ingredient in the essential oil of thyme is thymol, a potent antiseptic used as a fungicide and a preservative. I've even seen ground dried thyme listed as an ingredient in insecticides.

There are many ornamental thymes, all clothed with tiniest leaves, to choose from—common *(Thymus vulgaris)*, silver *(Thymus* x *citriodorus* 'Sil-

To make *herbal teas* or infusions straight from the garden is a simple pleasure. Use only organically grown herbs. If the leaves or flowers are fresh, usually a small handful is needed per cup, less—a teaspoon or two—if dried. Rosemary, lemon balm, peppermint, and sage teas are made from the leaves. Chamomile and pot marigold teas are brewed from the flower petals. Steep the tea in a teapot or place a saucer on top of the cup, allowing it to brew for five to ten minutes. Sugar and lemon can be added to improve the flavor.

ver Queen'), golden (*Thymus* x *citriodorus* 'Aureus'), and woolly *(Thymus pseudolanuginosus)* are some of my choices. I once visited a wonderful hillside garden planted with forty mat-forming cultivars of thyme. It didn't matter whether or not it was in bloom. The soft flower colors—faded purples, washed-out mauves, delicate pinks, and dusty whites—woven among the gold, silver, and greens of the foliage gave it the look of an antique wool tapestry. After a rain, the air was drenched with its clean and comforting breath.

I admit to not being able to distinguish much difference between the scents of the thyme I grow. I find all of them equally scented, pleasing, and refreshing. I particularly enjoy the woolly thyme I grow in a crack in a rock wall where I can easily pet it as I pass by. Even on a wintry day, when it wears its burgundy coat, its scent emerges clearly, and remains on my hand for hours. On the other hand, golden and silver thyme are wonderful simply to look at, when they are planted along a path and woven into a flower border. The silver thyme hugs the lavender; the golden thyme edges a purpled flowered nepeta. Tiny creeping thyme leaves will complement the larger leaves of lavender and feverfew.

Pennyroyal is another tough and rugged plant willing and able to be walked on. Its greeting is a pleasant whiff of peppermint. But be warned that it is a long-distance runner; it will scamper off in all directions, especially where you don't want it.

One of the lesser known herbs but one worthy of better acquaintance is the sweet herb, *Lippia dulcis*, which the ancient Aztecs used for sweetening foods. If rubbed, the leaves are not sweet, but smell like camphor without a hint of their sweetness. If eaten, however, they are as sweet as sugar. They can be picked and eaten right off the bush or served shredded on fruit. (However, don't eat too many: a flavor chemist, Rich Dufresne, pointed out to me that camphor makes up 53 percent of their essential oil; camphor is mildly toxic, and large amounts can be unhealthy.) There are many reasons for growing the sweet herb, among them the way its white flowers continue blooming through-

out the entire summer. The plant itself is a handsome creeper flattening its body over the brick border.

Sweet woodruff (*Galium odoratum* syn. *Asperula odorata*) is one of the most beautifully patterned ground covers. Its shiny oblong leaves grow in whorls around the stem and form intricate patterns of floating stars. But it is not tough enough for heavy traffic. It needs the close protection of stepping stones. In any case, the deciduous leaves release their scent of newly mown hay only when dried. I grow sweet woodruff for its delicate foliage and for its seasonal scent when the leaves are dying back in the fall.

Paths bordered with herbs and aromatics are as pleasant to walk along as those with the scent actually underfoot. The decorative foliage of many aromatics can be woven into a tapestry of color providing a medley of scent. The first plants that come to mind are the scented geraniums. Combining a wide selection of fragrances, foliage textures, and colors, they are a natural for lining a path. Today's choices of scented geraniums run into the hundreds, representing the widest range of scents in a plant genus. The rose-scented geraniums are among the most popular, but you can also get everything from fruit scents—apple, lemon, orange, grape, strawberry, coconut, and apricot—to such spices as cinnamon, nutmeg, ginger, and cloves, plus woody notes, like pine and incense cedar. Leaves may be large or small, in various shades of green, plain gold, or variegation (gold or silver), and many textures—crinkled, smooth, or furry.

In the Victorian age, ladies placed scented geraniums indoors along narrow passages or near a stairway where long gowns would brush against them as guests passed. Musty parlors too were freshened by scented geraniums. Plants growing on parlor windowsills were routinely ruffled before guests arrived so their fragrance would refresh the air.

I grow lemon-scented geraniums on the windowsill above my kitchen sink, where I can easily rub my hands on them after peeling onions or shrimp.

Degas' famous painting, *"Absinthe,"* graphically depicts the harm caused by drinking a bitter spirit concocted from wormwood (*Artemisia absinthium*) that contains 68 percent alcohol. When Pernod, the original version of an absinthe, was introduced in 1797, it became a popular drink until more than a hundred years later, when it was scientifically proven that repeatedly drinking absinthe caused delirium, hallucinations, and permanent mental illness. It was first banned in Switzerland, then France, and finally Spain in 1939. The absinthe-type liquor produced today is an imitation without the harmful effects.

The essential oil of the geranium stays on my hands, masking any unpleasant scent as well as, if not better than, lemon juice.

The silvery foliage of wormwood and lavender add light and sparkle as they deliver a pungent punch. The finely divided, silvery-gray foliage of wormwood, *Artemisia absinthium*, was worn as a charm by medieval travelers. It was believed to have powers of protection and, like smelling salts, its bracing aroma sustained the weary and kept them marching on their long pilgrimages. It is also the plant from which absinthe is distilled, making it, as Dr. Allan Armitage says, "the cause of much heartache and headache." Besides being strewn along with other herbs on floors to purify the air, wormwood was pinned on clothing to repel moths and hung from rafters in hopes it would ward off the plague. 'Lambrook Silver', an eighteen- to thirty-two-inch cultivar, is a handsome garden plant with graceful and delicately cut silver-gray foliage.

Today wormwood is grown more often for its silver foliage than for its scent. In the garden wormwood's silver foliage halos any plants it surrounds. And surround them it will. I mistakenly let it loose in my flower border before I realized how fast it could run. Now each spring I pull it out of the formal flower border whenever I see it, and the ones I miss provide just enough silver without crowding their neighbors. I took advantage of its fleet-footed nature when I purposely planted it on a bank with shrub roses. It quickly filled in so that weeding is rarely necessary. In the fall I gather its foliage and dry it for weaving into Christmas wreaths and mixing with fresh greens in holiday arrangements.

Lavender has long been cherished as a scent with multiple uses. As a perfume it has aided many a seduction. Cleopatra scented the sails of her barge with lavender water when she sailed to meet Mark Anthony. I

Lavender bottles are an old-fashioned way to scent drawers, closets, and rooms to keep them fresh and sweet-smelling. They are called bottles because the flower heads are encased by the stems to prevent the flowers from dropping off into the linens. To make one, twenty long stems of lavender, fully open and freshly picked, are needed. Tie the flower heads with a green thread in a bundle at their necks. Bend each stem gently back, over the flower heads to encase the flowers. When freshly picked, the stems are flexible enough to bend without breaking. When they are all bent back, arrange them neatly and tie again with a thin ribbon just below the flower bundle. The ends of the ribbon can be tied in a bow or woven around in and out of the stems and tied at the bottom. Allow the bottles to dry naturally before placing them in drawers or closets.

think of it as the original air freshener, since in the seventeenth century, lavender was one of the most popular flowers used to purge the stink from London's streets. Its presence was also believed to ward off the plague.

I personally find the lavender family is a confusing mix of Latin, common, and cultivar names, especially since the family resemblance is so strong. All of the flowers are easily identified as lavender, but the proper species is often hard to place. Today English lavender, the source of the classic lavender scent, is identified as *Lavandula angustifolia*, but formerly it was known as *L. officinalis*, *L. spica*, and *L. vera*. Your guess is as good as mine as what it will be called tomorrow. The Spanish lavender—*L. stoechas*, last time I checked—is the only one whose name I can be counted on to get right. It is distinct, with its small violet flowers clustered together at the top of the stem, looking a little like a pinecone, and topped by larger purple "rabbit ears." I'll never forget seeing clumps of it growing on a sandy beach in Portugal.

Owing to their long history of cultivation, today's garden lavenders are most often hybrids and cultivars. Knowing their names is not as important as in other families, since they are all wonderfully scented. In fact, all parts of the plants are endowed with the pungent, invigorating, and reviving scent. I have picked heavily scented foliage dusted with snow in winter, and its scent has remained on my hands for hours. Typically the flowers are lavender-blue, but white, pink, and purple flowers are also available. I have a mix of a half dozen different lavenders, and they are all very productive spreading bushes that have grown fat in their lean soil. It is only my passion for more flowers that keeps me from planting dwarf varieties. I prefer to harvest blooms in early summer for bouquets and to scent my closets without completely depleting the bushes. Lavender, however, doesn't stop blooming after its first glorious flush, but sporadically flowers on until frost unless hit by high humidity and oppressive heat. Even so, its silver foliage is a wonderful edging for a path, border to a bed or ground cover under roses.

Lavender is the oil famous for treating and healing burns. The story often told is of one of the founding fathers of aromatherapy, Dr. R. M. Gattefossé, who burned himself severely in his laboratory, then accidentally plunged his hand into the nearest bowl, which was filled with essential oil of lavender. His pain ceased and the burn quickly healed.

Providing strong contrast in a garden bed, different shades of purple mimic shadows. Purple basil is a natural with its ruffled reddish purple leaves. Its taller relative, purple perila, fits more easily into the middle and back of the border. Bronze fennel (*Foeniculum vulgare* 'Purpureum') provides an anise scent and a delightful flutter of threadlike foliage.

The various mints and lemon balm *(Melissa officinalis)* have scents loved by many. As noted, I resent their aggressive ways, although the more decorative varieties can be planted in pots at the entrance to a path to give the path definition. My first choice is *Mentha suaveolens* 'Variegata', the pineapple mint, with its sweet fruity scent and its green leaves edged in wide bands of white. Occasionally an all-white leaf or even a white stem appears for a more dramatic coloration. The lemon balm 'All Gold' will brighten a shady spot with its gold leaves, and 'Aurea' does the same with its golden variegated leaves. Both are beautiful. Combine a bunch in an oversized pot and let them slug it out.

Lavender cotton, *Santolina chamaecyparissus*, has a texture like sea coral tarnished to a silver gray. Solitary yellow button flowers bloom in summer. It is a bitter herb with a pungent yet spicy scent reputed to keep bugs at bay. *S. virens*, green lavender cotton, is similarly scented, with a ferny, deep green foliage that also forms a mound two feet high. They both grow densely and compactly and are frequently used to border an herb garden or to make knot garden hedges.

Many of the American native salvias are hard to find but worth the search. Pineapple sage and Mexican sage are two of my favorites. *Salvia elegans* has pineapple-scented red spike flowers and is one of the last flowers to bloom in my garden. I admit I grow it as much for its red flowers as for its pineapple scent, but I like a sprig of pineapple sage in iced tea, with a flavor sweeter than the more commonly used mint. I pick bits of foliage all summer long to add to summer drinks. The plants are quick growers and will probably be five feet high and almost as wide by summer's end. I've never noticed that cutting pieces of foliage has slowed it down much. One plant is probably all a garden needs, but I usually plant several in different locations so I can gather the flowers in the fall. If the weather is cooperative, I often have bouquets for Thanksgiving. The slightly taller Mexican sage, *Salvia leucantha*, has large plumes covered in cashmere-soft purple calyces to highlight the small white angora flowers. To some people, the smell is like something you wish you hadn't stepped in. Tovah Martin smells "burnt cocoa"; other garden visitors have simply called it woodsy, nutty, or fruity. It is one of the best salvias for dried flower arrangements—I have kept dried bunches for two years. It blooms for several months in the garden. Last year I cut back a plant and brought it into the greenhouse where it continued to bloom off and on all winter. Even though this salvia grows very large by October, it is not difficult to fit into a small garden if surrounded by annual herbs that finish first. Dill and borage are obvious choices. Basil stays longer but doesn't like the cold weather and quits before the salvia blooms. Scented geraniums are another good partner, since I usually dig them up and bring them inside in September.

It goes without saying that fragrant flowers can be added to the aromatic mix. Scented annuals, perennials, and bulbs can be planted together with aromatics in a border alongside the path. A scented shrub might well stand at the opening of the path, or flank it; as they grow, the shrubs will focus the attention of the stroller and invite him or her down the perfumed path. If the shrub is balsam, it too will scent the air for all who brush against it.

Another place to play with aromatics is on a stone or brick terrace. There's no need to plant only creepers; taller plants can sprout up at random, adding a luxurious look. On a terrace there is more than one route to take, and it is easy to avoid stepping on taller plants. A chair or table can be moved around to avoid being placed over a plant or can be playfully placed to shade a plant or placed with one leg actually in a plant. (That will make a visitor pause. I know from experience.)

The grass in the enclosed area beside our carriage house was permanently disfigured by ruts from the kids' bikes, the spillover of projects from the carpentry shop, and a table and chairs that had sat too long in one spot. We hit upon the idea of replacing the grass with cobblestones—much more in keeping with the mood of the house. We enlarged the straight six-foot-wide flower borders to eight feet, and the large stones gave them a friendlier, informal, irregular edge. Before laying the stones, we added several inches of sand to help the drainage and support the stones. The spaces between them, filled with pockets of topsoil, turned out to be perfect for such aromatic herbs as thyme, pennyroyal, chives, and oregano. As these spilled over the rocks, the hard edges of the yard softened. Fragrance rose to greet us wherever we stepped, so we added more perfumed flowers and tall aromatics to brush against—sweet peas, alyssum, pinks, lavenders, nepeta, and flowering tobacco *(Nicotiana alata)*, as well as assorted miniature bulbs. The thymes have proven to be the true workhorses of this garden—they can be trod on, they suppress weeds, and are evergreen, adding a rosy glow to the stones in winter.

If you're adventurous, you might try duplicating the old-fashioned stone benches often found in historic English gardens, with their seats planted with herbs for the guests to sit on. Modern versions made from wood add whimsy, along with a comforting fragrance, to a cozy corner of the garden.

a scented lawn
If you are tired of mowing a lawn, you might consider a radical solution: Replace a section of lawn with tough herbs. The clean, fresh odor of a lawn being mowed is the most familiar garden fragrance in America, but grass is scentless when walked on. A chamomile lawn, on the other hand, releases an applelike fragrance every time it is touched. It is all too rare a pleasure. Whenever I smell chamomile, I remember—with a mixture of pleasure, awe, and jealousy—walking across Ray Reddell's chamomile lawn in the center of his fragrance garden in Petaluma, California.

Chamomile lawns were popular in Tudor times; Shakespeare refers to Falstaff's wont to walk upon them. There is one today in the garden of Buckingham Palace. The earliest description of a grass lawn being grown was in 1613, but grass did not overtake chamomile as the favorite ground cover until the eighteenth century, partly because of the difficulty of getting good grass seed. A chamomile lawn need not be lost in history. It is planted with Roman

chamomile, *Chamaemelum nobile*, not to be confused with *Matricaria recutita*, the German chamomile. It is easy to mix these up. Both chamomiles are used for making tea, have an applelike scent and daisylike flowers, but here the similarity stops. They are not botanically related. Roman chamomile is a perennial that creeps, is drought-resistant, and can be mowed. German chamomile grows erect, six to eighteen inches high, and is an annual.

Establishing a Roman chamomile lawn is similar to seeding a grass lawn. Weeding is necessary through the first year, as is regular rolling. By the second year, the plants become established enough to suppress weeds and then can be walked and sat on. It needs only to be rolled in the fall and mowed twice a year. The disadvantage for Americans is that football, golf, and soccer cannot be played on a chamomile lawn.

> A warm, not hot, steeped *chamomile* tea bag will reduce facial puffiness and help in treating acne, eczema, dermatitis, and boils. The essential oil from chamomile flowers contains azulene, an anti-inflammatory agent. However, commercially, chamomile owes its claim to fame to its popular use in shampoos and rinses. It can lighten and soften hair when an infusion is used as a final rinse.

drying herbs
Thoreau wrote about picking the young tips of the balsam fir, *Abies balsamea*, and putting them in his pocket. When he took them out a few days later they reminded him of the fragrance of strawberries, though "somewhat more aromatic and spicy." In the confined warmth of his pocket, the essential oils of the fir tips emerged and became concentrated as the tips themselves dried out.

There are flowers and herbs that develop a more pronounced scent as they fade or even after drying. The smell of the drying foliage of violets, sweet woodruff, and strawberry leaves are the "sweet good-byes of the garden year"; almost as if knowing that their time has come, they send forth their sweetest scent in one last all-out effort. The flowers of lesser calamint, *Calamintha nepeta*, retain their mint scent after frost as they die on the stems. I have gathered the dried flowers in February and found the scent still strong.

In our camp in the Adirondacks we have several small pillows stuffed with dried balsam that I tuck behind the larger pillows on the sofa. Unwit-

tingly, guests sit down and lean back on the pillow, releasing the wonderful, fresh, woodsy scent. Their reaction is always the same. They comment on how wonderful it smells to be in the woods and how marvelous that even sitting inside they can enjoy it—they think that the balsam scent is seeping in under the doors and around the window frames.

Stuffing pillows with dried herbs is hardly new. Nero used rose-petal-stuffed pillows for his guests to recline on at his famous banquets. Mugwort, *Artemisia vulgaris*, was dried and stuffed in pillows to improve sleep and was believed to induce prophetic dreams. Not for me, though—the aroma of mugwort would more likely keep me awake. I find its pungent scent bracing, more suitable for repelling moths then attracting sleep. I prefer rose petals, which in any event have probably always been the most popular substance for scenting pillows. Today's gardeners can easily do this: slip dried or fresh rose petals between a pillow and its case, then enjoy the scent as you drift off at night and again when you wake in the morning.

Although fewer and fewer personal letters are written today, if you place a fragrant flower or aromatic leaf in a letter before sealing it, the scent gains potency as it travels to surprise the recipient with a wispy pungent kiss.

harvesting herbs for drying The best
time to harvest herbs is just before flowering or when the flowers are beginning to open. It is then that herbs have the highest concentration of oils in their leaves and last the longest. They should be harvested when the leaves are the most turgid, just after the dew dries on a sunny morning. Rinse them off, pat them dry, and hang them for a complete drying, using the same methods as you would for drying flowers. Flowers that air-dry, such as lavender and rosebuds, can be mixed in to add color.

I gather culinary herbs in bunches, a half dozen or more stems together, stretch a rubber band around them, and hang them upside down. As they dry, the rubber band contracts and holds the herbs together. The bundles can be made from a single herb or a mixture.

A bouquet garni, a mixture of herbs tied together in a bundle suitable for use in a pot, is a cook's delight. The classic ingredients are thyme, parsley, and a bay leaf; celery leaves are often added, and tarragon and sage are optional. Traditionally, a freshly picked or dried bouquet garni is simmered in a stockpot to flavor soups or is laid under a roast before cooking, flavoring the meat as well as the gravy. Dried herbs are best used for cooking within six months, but their fragrance will last longer.

Drying takes only a few days—just until the leaves crinkle. I tie some bundles onto a wire wreath form to decorate the kitchen. The dried herbs for cooking can be chopped and stored in a jar or can be stored in their original bundles inside airtight containers to use for winter flavorings. They are also decorative hung in a kitchen to dry and use later. If they get too old or dusty, burn them on top of coals to add flavor to a barbecue or lay them on a smoldering fire on a dreary winter day to release their cheerfully pungent smoke.

When lavender is dry, it holds its scent for three years. Gathered into nosegays or made into the lavender wands popular in France, it can be laid on a table or placed in a drawer to scent linens. The stems of lavender, thyme, or both can be bundled together and lit to smolder and burn like incense; this was once a popular way to dispel mustiness. On a cold winter day, herbs steeped in an open teapot waft a fragrant steam of refreshing aroma and moisture into a dry room.

Most *essential oils* are not used full strength but are diluted in carrier oil such as soy or grapeseed. Carrier oil should be pure and have little or no smell of its own. The best oils are cold-pressed so they retain their essential vitamin content. If you make your own oils you can be sure of the quality by using homegrown and pesticide-free plants. You will also save money. Lavender and chamomile flowers, thyme, rosemary, sage, and marjoram leaves are good choices to start with. Use eight ounces of a fresh herb or four ounces of dried herb per pint of oil (if fresh herbs are used, wash and dry them). Place the herbs in a clear glass bottle and completely cover them with the oil. Seal the bottle tightly and place it on a sunny windowsill for two to three weeks. Then strain the oil to remove the herbs and decant into dark bottles for storage. The oil is now ready for use as massage oil, bath oil, or room perfume.

potpourri
Today we don't have as great a need as we once did to disguise unpleasant odors. So potpourri is used in the home to add to the aura of warmth and welcome—a luxury item, no longer a necessity.

Rose petals are the most popular ingredient, in spite of the fact that they lose their scent when they are dry. This doesn't matter, because most of the long-lasting scent of potpourri comes not from the petals themselves, but from the drops of essential oils—purchased from gift or craft shops or drugstore—that are added both when combining the ingredients and again later whenever the potpourri needs refreshing. The essential oils have been painstakingly extracted from the plants and cover a wide range of fragrances and prices.

Buy the essential oil of the fragrance you like best and add a drop or two to your favorite petals or whole dried flowers. Any petals can be scented to smell like rose, lavender, or jasmine by putting a few drops of oil on the mixture, stirring gently, sealing in a jar or plastic bag, and storing away from direct sunlight until ready to use.

My potpourri consists mostly of rose petals, gathered throughout the summer and decorated with rosebuds picked when frost is expected in the fall. For contrasting color, I sometimes add blue lavender and yellow calendula. Experiment to see what you like. You can't go wrong if you buy a scent that pleases you.

6 the rogues

love 'em or hate 'em Fragrances are as subject to whims and fads as clothes. Their popularity varies with the times as well as the culture. An optimistic recommendation from an antique French book was to "rub thy face with violets and goat's milk and there is not a prince in the world who will not follow thee." (Having a couple of single daughters, duty compels me to pass along helpful hints as I come upon them.)

Usually, controversial fragrances emerge when sweet, heavy-scented flowers are confined in a room. Many of the flowers I have classed as seductresses have scents that cross over and become offensive when confined in small spaces or when you bury your nose in a blossom. In too great intensity, other elements of their makeup are revealed. These elements are not necessarily unpleasant in themselves, but in this concentrated state people react to them differently. The offensive elements tend to be mossy, earthy, or musty, or dizzyingly sweet—for example, the strong, heady smell of paperwhite daffodils. A bowl of paperwhites placed in a living room will scent every adjoining room as well. During the day the fragrance is not powerful enough to be controversial; but come nightfall, the fragrance increases and takes on a hint of mothballs. Some people feel strongly enough about this characteristic to banish them at dusk to an out-of-the-way place until morning. Paperwhites can divide a crowd. People are either delighted by them or find them cloying or sickly sweet. Almost no one can be neutral in the face of such a strong scent.

"[The lily] was lord of all it surveyed by virtue of its scent and striking appearance. Yet, her mother would sometimes call from her chair, 'Close the garden gate a little, the lilies are making the drawing room uninhabitable.'"

—Colette

Scents like these can be confusing. I remember one Christmas Eve when my eldest daughter, Margaret, hurriedly grabbed me and pulled me into the dining room before the guests arrived. She was sure the puppy had had an accident, but she couldn't find it. As you have probably guessed, the paperwhites were the culprit, not the dog.

Another spoiler that has only to be brought indoors to offend is the mayflower, or trailing arbutus, *Epigaea repens*. A sweetly scented woodland flower, it produces a distinctly unpleasant smell in the house.

Hyacinths, in particular, are seductresses with a heavy perfume that after a few days indoors "goes off" (as florists say). This happens as the flowers are fading, so if their perfume begins to offend, they can be tossed out. The same is true of tuberoses, a favorite for the traditional Hawaiian lei. Rayford Reddell, a nursery owner and rose expert, notes that you could be due for a shock if you bury your nose in an otherwise welcoming lei: you may well "detect an unmistakable hint of putrefaction."

Florists report that customers often request that fragrant lilies be omitted from their arrangements. Many people find that their scent, poured forth in such excess, all at once, becomes too sickeningly sweet and pervasive indoors. A single lily can overwhelm a room.

Valerian, *Valeriana officinalis*, has a heliotropelike breath in the garden but an underlying unpleasantness when smelled up close. Its roots have a stronger smell and are responsible for one of valerian's common names, "phew plant." The plant contains valeric acid, a compound also found in human perspiration. Consequently a clump of valerian on a warm day has been described as smelling like a postgame locker room, although the flowers are pretty enough, looking a little like Queen Anne's lace on stilts. I have it growing in an area where I often sit and read, and I've never found its odor offensive, although its habit of stampeding wildly over neighboring plants might well be described that way.

The smell of boxwood, especially after a shower, can be either stimulating or disturbing. Oliver Wendell Holmes thought it the most memory-stirring of all scents. To garden designer Conni Cross's nose, boxwood is "cat urine," and she is adamant in her conviction that nobody can honestly find any other odor in it. (Her explanation of why some people like it is that it is an "acquired taste.")

Clary sage *(Salvia sclarea)* is another overpowering scent, though not one sweet enough to fall into the seductress category. J. Barry Ferguson says, "It smells of perspiration, a coal miner's armpit. Nice ladies blush and look away." Marco Polo Stufano calls its odor "foxy." Tovah Martin finds its foliage "fruit-scented." "Cat urine," "a hospital ward," "household cleaner," and "antiseptic" are other descriptions. Yet from a distance, clary is always admired for its beauty. Strangely, its essential oil finds use as a fixative in perfume-making when synthetic substitutes are mixed with genuine floral essences. Its presence stabilizes the combination, which would otherwise break down in a month. Another of its uses is as a flavoring in muscatel wine and in adding woody, amber notes to tobacco.

Personally, I like the looks of clary sage. It is bold, broad, and statuesque. Small white, pink, or lilac flowers completely cover the many-branched flowering stems, which stand three feet tall. I wouldn't place it next to a path where its controversial perfume might offend a guest, but then again, you never know. Its stems are sticky to the touch and it's certain that anyone who grabs it will want to wash. Planted back a few feet from a path or in a border, it is one of the delights of midsummer.

With some flowers it isn't their scent but their associations that are their undoing. Just as stephanotis is "the wedding flower," flowers such as tuberoses and gladiolus are frequently included in funeral bouquets, and so are often excluded from gardens or decorative arrangements. This is a pity; don't be too hasty to reject a fragrant flower. Many a flower I disliked at one time has later become a valued companion.

If you go outside this country, you'll discover even more scents tainted by association. In Europe, wintergreen is a common fragrance in toilet cleaners. This may be why you won't find wintergreen-flavored toothpaste or candies in England or other European countries. I love the scent; ever since Life Savers came into my life I think of them whenever I pick a leaf of wintergreen *(Gaultheria procumbens)* while walking in a woodland. I often chew on a leaf or split it to breathe its refreshing scent.

The Masai women on the East African plains use cow dung as a hair gel. When I visited Africa in the 1960s, I found this repugnant. It wasn't until we took the family to Tavern on the Green, a New York City restaurant in Central Park, on the occasion of my oldest daughter's graduation from high school, that I changed my mind. As we were getting out of the taxi, my cousin remarked on the wonderful smell. My eleven-year-old son piped up. "Aunt Puddy," he said, "that's horse manure." Which of course it was. But to Aunt Puddy, who had at first failed to recognize it out of the context of her garden, it was a beautiful scent. She spreads it on her roses twice a year and it does wonders. The smell of manure also stirs pleasant memories in equestrians. We are not as different from the Masai as we think.

Other flowers that launch controversy on a summer's breeze include the garden phlox, *Phlox paniculata.* It reminds Joe Eck of urine and his garden design partner, Wayne Winterrowd, of his grandmother's face powder. "Peppery" is another common description, or "peppery and pigsty." Perhaps one explanation is that different essential oils evaporate at different rates. The fragrance of phlox changes as it ages from pleasant to unpleasant.

Nevertheless, phlox is the mainstay of my late summer border, with the brightest clusters of bloom in assorted pinks, purples, and whites. Butterflies too are happy with my choice and spend hours searching out their nectar. As is often the case with phlox, when I first planted them I had many varieties that were susceptible to powdery mildew. It was simply through an unconscious selection process that I haven't had a problem with mildew in years. Varieties that were susceptible were pulled out and ones that stood the test of heat and humidity flourished, filling in the empty spaces.

Bugbane, *Cimicifuga,* is named for the scent of its leaves, which supposedly drives bugs away. Three commonly grown garden varieties, *C. sim-*

plex ramosa 'Atropurpurea', *C. simplex*, and *C. racemosa*, while differing in height, all have similar looking flowers. *C. simplex* grows the shortest, three to four feet high; *C. simplex ramosa* 'Atropurpurea' fits in the middle, at four to six feet tall, while *C. racemosa* reaches up to eight feet. These graceful woodland plants send up tall feathery white jets well above the foliage. Glowing in the dark the flowers resemble fairy candles, another of their common names, with elegant spires of tiny white flowers lining the top of the stalk. The only way I can tell *C. racemosa* and *C. simplex* apart is by their time of bloom, the first July through August and the other late September and October. However, *C. simplex ramosa* 'Atropurpurea' is easily distinguished by its dark purplish stems and foliage. It also has a lovely sweet breath. *C. simplex* 'White pearl' smells like tuberoses, and *C. racemosa* smells like stagnant water or lily-of-the-valley, depending on whom you ask.

There are no surprises here. The varying perceptions are typical of the human race. Smells are personal. Each of us has his or her likes and dislikes and our own way of reacting to the unpredictable invisible stimuli that enter our noses.

the nose twisters "Nose twisters" is the name coined
by Louise Beebe Wilder for flowers and foliage with a pungent breath. Smelling them is a bit like sniffing pepper. Their scents are sharp, nose-tickling, sometimes bitter. Wormwood, for example, is bitterly aromatic, as is the golden-leaved feverfew, while the tang of chrysanthemums and bluebeard *(Caryopteris sp.)* becomes all too evident when their leaves are pinched.

Many of these pungent scents have been used as insect repellents and as an alternative to mothballs. Despite the availability of chemical products, some work so well that they are still used for these purposes. Cotton lavender *(Santolina chamaecyparissus)* is a handsome plant with yellow button flowers held in large heads and gray, tightly curled foliage that gleams like pewter. I prefer its odor to that of mothballs and tuck pieces of the foliage in drawers instead.

"Hot smells" is how Wayne Winterrowd describes the Nose Twisters. "The one that exists most strongly in my memory is lantana," he writes, "which self-seeded all over my grandmother's gardens, usually in the orange-yellow, but sometimes in lavender-cream. What a strange dusty odor. I don't grow that plant any more, but I cannot pass it, in a nursery or in someone else's garden, without remembering. Marigolds, too, which really are the quintessence of summer, however one might feel about them otherwise. Nasturtiums, too, which we never ate, for in my part of the South one never ate anything that was not cooked to death, never planted, either, for many things in my grandmother's garden just came up. Tomato leaves, and the curious, musty odor of gourd leaves. I mean to say that gourd leaves smelled exactly like my great-grandmother's room. She was bedridden and had no mind, but we visited her often in her room, and it had that same musty smell, of very old people."

Infusions made from the dried or fresh petals of pot marigold, *Calendula officinalis*, can be applied directly to the face as toners and used in soaking compresses to calm the itchy eyes of hay fever.

Lantana is another old reliable, even in my northern garden, where I only grow it in pots and window boxes. The pots I move into the greenhouse, where they bloom continuously all winter, and I pick the flowers for miniature arrangements. The window boxes filled with blue lantana are a pleasure, as they don't mind if they are forgotten from time to time in the frenzy of watering. The blue flowers beautifully spill over the edge of the boxes and grow several feet long before frost notifies me that it's time to take them in. Although flaunted in the trade as a blue lantana, it is really purple. I know, because purple combines well with anything. It was my daughter Margaret who opened my eyes to the color purple's versatility. For months after her fifth birthday she refused to get dressed unless she could wear something purple. She flatly stated that purple goes with everything. Given so little choice in the matter, I accepted her premise and have never regretted it.

Most marigolds have a rough, strong scent. In *Cooking from the Garden*, Rosalind Creasy calls the scent of marigolds "somewhere between skunk and quinine." She does, however, approve of the scent of the lemon and orange

Gem Hybrids; two signet marigolds *(Tagetes tenuifolia)* that taste like their namesakes. She even recommends cooking with them.

There are, of course, plenty of scentless marigolds. Most of them date back to the time sixty years or so ago, when, with marigolds at the height of their popularity as popular bedding plants, people who disliked marigolds because of their scent complained to seedsman David Burpee. Since his own favorite flowers were marigolds, he enlisted the help of plant breeders in developing a scentless variety. An odorless marigold had been discovered in China in 1930 by a missionary who sent seeds to Burpee, and the scentless marigolds of today are descendants of that Chinese sport. Oddly, marigolds are native to the Americas, not Asia, so someone must have taken them to China in the first place.

dual personalities
The dual-scented plants send mixed messages, one sweet scent usually coming from their flowers and another, sharp and offensive, hiding in their leaves. It seems the plants are at war with themselves (not unlike some people I know). When they are left alone, only the fragrance is evident and their beauty shines. But ruffle their foliage or attempt to move them, and they cause a stink.

These plants with warring scents are nature's dual personalities. Their pleasant perfume lifts the spirits while their foul odor brings the sniffer back down. It can be a bumpy ride.

Spring starflowers *(Ipheion uniflorum)*, angel's trumpets *(Datura sp.)*, and society garlic *(Tulbaghia violacea variegata)* are three of the better known members of this group. Both spring starflower and society garlic have flowers with a sweet mint fragrance, but their leaves, when bruised, release an odor of onion and garlic. For more than six weeks, the spring starflowers send up stems, each with a starry light blue flower. Their floppy, grassy leaves appear in the fall and stay through the winter, disappearing only after the spring flowers have bloomed.

Society garlic also has thin, grasslike leaves arching from the center of the plant and sometimes curling at the ends. Each green strand is edged with white, blushing to pink as they converge near the soil. When the leaves are stroked, a slight garlic scent can be noticed, but if a leaf is broken or a browned strand removed, a strong garlic scent emerges. The soft purple flowers are sweetly scented when smelled up close. Undisturbed, the plant is innocently fragrant, its beautiful leaves and sweet flower scent making it a garlic to be accepted in polite society.

But it can cause trouble. Two friends who live in a remote part of the Northeast once told me about how they had made the mistake of buying a plant of society garlic in California and trying to bring it back with them. They had to abandon it (discreetly, one hopes) at the airport in Chicago, halfway home: they could no longer bear its stink—what they described as "rancid onions"—let alone suffer the glares of fellow passengers. The devil in me got to thinking: Could this be a solution to the problem of hurrying dawdling guests along at the end of a party—shake a plant of society garlic?

Many alliums (also members of the onion family) have sweetly scented flowers and foliage with the odor of raw onions. *Allium ramosum* was formerly known as *A. odorum* because of its sweet scent. The blossoms of *A. neapolitanum* have a faintly pleasant scent, not unlike freesias, and are sold as a cut flower in Europe. Their clear white dainty flowers are pretty enough, so it is easy to keep their family connections a secret, and their identity frequently goes undetected. I grow many varieties of alliums, some in flower borders and some in the herb garden, more for their ornamental flowers than their scent. When I pick the dried ornamental seed heads, they are scentless.

Primula auricula visosa is another plant with fragrant purple flowers and rank-smelling foliage. The harlequin glorybower, *Clerodendrum trichotomum fargesii*, has jasmine-scented white flowers, as I mentioned earlier. What I forgot to tell you is the leaves carry the roast beef smell of *Iris foetidissima*.

While there are more dual-personality flowers than you might think, the flowers of many of them are too beautiful and too pleasantly fragrant to ignore. I don't shy away from growing them. My advice is simply to treat them with kid gloves and stay a respectful distance away. Plant them back from paths where their leaves aren't likely to be touched or ruffled. And do not in any circumstances attempt to cut them for bouquets unless you're a practical joker who enjoys creating havoc and a little merriment.

the stinkers

Bad odors are often difficult to avoid. Smells literally get up our noses, mostly without our consent. Nobody goes out of their way to inhale the stench from skunk, rotting garbage, or decaying fish. In extreme cases, such smells can make you retch and recoil. Even holding your nose is not enough. So it follows that we wouldn't purposely plant something that smells bad. Yet in a few cases there are reasons to include what I call a stinker in your garden: it may be their beauty, it may be their color or texture, or it may be simply because the plant is odd enough to amuse me.

Usually the plants with foul odors in their leaves are discreet, like skunks. If you don't disturb them, they won't offend. Foul odors in foliage probably serve to discourage the depredations of insects and pests, while a rank scent in a flower tends to attract pollinators. Such flowers are frequently colored dull red, purple, or brown, shaded to look like decaying meat.

A prime example is the voodoo lily of northwest India *(Sauromatum guttatum)*. Its spathe—it wouldn't be fair to call it a flower—is on a one- to two-foot stalk with a drooping, somewhat twisted blade of the same length. It is a greenish purple color on the outside and green with irregular blotches of purple inside, somewhat like the marbleized markings on raw meat. For two or three days after the flower matures, it emits the strong, foul odor of putrid flesh. It can be grown as a houseplant easily enough, and will bloom if the tuber is placed in a bowl of water rather than soil. But during its first days of bloom you'll have to banish it from the house.

Another common woodland plant with brown flowers and marbled markings, and to some an unpleasant odor, is the *Trillium erectum* of North America. I have it naturalized along our woodland path where its chocolate flowers contrast attractively with the surrounding greens. One of its common

names is the stinking trillium. In fact, however, I have not found its peculiar odor offensive—you only notice it up close. Most trilliums are completely odorless. Appropriately, flies and ants pollinate it.

Dutchman's pipe, *Aristolochia durior*, has large heart-shaped leaves that overlap like shingles to hide the yawning mouth of its small, pipe-shaped flowers. When insects enter the flowers, downward-pointing hairs trap them. The insects have no choice but to stay there, feasting on the nectar and accumulating pollen. After the nectar is consumed, the stigma withers and the hairs relax, allowing the insect—carrying the pollen—to leave. The flowers emit an odd odor, not entirely unpleasant. I grow the plant for its beautiful leaves and have noticed the odor only when I've gone looking for it. J. Barry Ferguson, a renowned flower designer, grows Dutchman's pipe in the most interesting way: it climbs over an arch between two buildings and along the way wreaths the neck of a sculptured horse head. I'm reminded of the victor of the Kentucky Derby whenever I see it.

Crown imperial *(Fritillaria imperialis)* has a beautiful flower with a bad case of halitosis—as Christopher Lloyd says, "a disconcerting mixture of garlic and foxy." A stroller through the garden rarely notices the odor of the flowers, since they bloom when the weather is cool. Only the gardener knows of their bad breath. If you stay at arm's length and never pluck them, they can be admired for their beauty alone. That's one reason I plant them three feet or more back from our woodland path. The bulbs are smellier than their flowers, which makes planting a trying process. There is no escape until the job is done. When planting crown imperials, it is a good idea to wear gloves, as the bulbs have been known to cause a skin rash. These fritillaries don't like wet, and it is only in drier areas with good drainage that they have naturalized. To make sure the bulbs stay on the dry side in summer when they are dormant, I place a few inches of grit or gravel underneath them.

The beauty of the flower made me determined to find an acceptable way of including them in an arrangement. I finally succeeded this spring when I combined a single crown imperial with a dozen strongly scented daffodils. No one who came for dinner noticed the odor. A dozen hyacinths works too.

I was amused to see a large bunch of crown imperial for sale in a fancy Fifth Avenue florist in New York City. They weren't refrigerated but sat prominently on a table. I watched for a while as customers came in and commented on their beauty. Sales were indeed brisk. Finally, I could contain myself no longer. I asked the clerk how he could stand to spend the day confined in a room with their pervasive bad breath. He admitted it was tough. The customers apparently didn't connect the bad odor to the crown imperial, and in any case were too polite to comment. They probably thought another customer had forgotten his deodorant.

"Skunk cabbage" aptly describes both the appearance—cabbagelike foliage—and foul smell of *Symplocarpus foetidus*. The oddly shaped hooded and mottled flowers are unusual and arresting in flower arrangements. The trick I learned from J. Barry Ferguson is to set the flowers in water outside the back door for ten minutes, so they "ain't misbehavin'" when you bring them inside. Often a tablespoon of household bleach added to the water helps. Their foul odor disappears. Both are beautiful flowers whose reputation has been tainted by their bad breath. In an arrangement, they may startle gardening guests surprised to see them so well-behaved. In a wild garden near a pond or a distance from a path, I find them an attractive ground cover.

The most offensive plant I wrestle with is *Houttuynia cordata* 'Chameleon', known as the chameleon plant. I first thought it a sweet little thing when we purchased it, lured by the exaggerated descriptions of its beauty and usefulness in a catalog: "An outstanding, attention-grabbing, new ground cover from Korea with heart-shaped foliage of yellow, green, bronze and scarlet red. Tiny white flowers bloom in the summer. Makes a vigorous growing mat of 6 to 9 inches in height." Other catalogs echoed this praise. Not one mentioned the plant's vile smell and its unstoppable tendency to spread. "Vigorous growing mat," indeed! Succumbing to the description, I ordered a half dozen starts.

Its true nature soon revealed itself. When I tried to confine it, remove it, or put a stop to its aggressive travels, I found its roots traveled as quickly underground as vines do above. It turned out to be as difficult to eradicate as poison ivy. The first time I weeded out a small patch, I didn't wear gloves, and its foul odor contaminated my hands. Even though I washed them with soap, soaked them in ammonia and household bleach, rubbed with a cleanser, and finished up with lemon juice before taking a shower, nothing removed nor masked the chameleon plant's stench. Instead I only piled on other odors, ammonia and lemon in particular. Needless to say, no one asked me to dance that evening.

Conni Cross, a garden designer, has compared the chameleon plant's odor to a dead rat left decaying under the porch. A neighbor of mine whose husband brought it home from a local nursery found it so vile that she nicknamed it "vomit vine." When she tried to pull it out, the odor permeated the air and nauseated her. She was reduced to wearing a hospital mask when trying to eradicate it.

I tried the J. Barry Ferguson remedy for skunk cabbage, cutting the gaudy foliage and leaving it to soak in a bucket of cold water. I checked in ten minutes, but the odor remained. I checked again in an hour; then repeatedly until the next day. Each time the odor seemed to be getting stronger and worse. Ten days later, its stench still rose up to greet me. Perversely, the foliage and flowers exhibited an amazing staying power. They still looked freshly cut after ten days. Chameleon plant strikes me as being a perfect candidate for breeders to test their skills in removing odors, although it would help to have training first as a pathologist immune to the odor of corpses.

Nowadays, whenever I walk along the path where chameleon plants grow, I am filled anew with remorse. Luckily, I planted it in a shady area, where it grows less vigorously than in full sun. The battle is not as fierce as it could be. I'm happy to report that if it is undisturbed, never touched, broken, or dug up, you probably won't be bothered by its smell. Recently I read that *Houttuynia cordata* is prized in Asian cooking for adding an orange-coriander aroma. I can only wonder if we are all growing the same plant.

There are other plants with body odor. The flowering currant, *Ribes rosceum*, is said to smell like tomcats. The rose family contains a number of plants with evil smells in their leaves. Hawthorn, cotoneaster, privet, and pyracantha each contain trimethylamine, which is also present in fish brine and occurs in the early stages of putrefaction. They are members of the aminoid group that give off a sweet-fishy odor when inhaled at close range. About ramson or wild garlic *(Allium ursinum)* and ramp or wild leek *(Allium tricoccum)* it has been said they "make the air hum with the smell of garlic in the spring." The pineapple lily, *Eucomis bicolor*, is named for its appearance, not its scent. It resembles a pineapple on a stick. I liken a close whiff to the unappetizing aroma of stewing cabbage. About the common Russian sage, *Perovskia atriplicifolia*, Dr. Allan Armitage writes, "In spite of the less-than-overwhelming flower size and the odor of foot soldiers' boots when the leaves are crushed, the species is a favorite of gardeners everywhere." It is a favorite in our garden in early fall for the small light purple flowers that cover its stems.

The stinking hellebore, *Helleborus foetidus*, reputedly emits a foul smell when you pick the flowers or bruise the foliage. But compared to the crown imperial, it is really a stinker only in name. So far as I am concerned, hellebores are an important part of chasing winter away. Nothing else blooms as long and puts up with whatever late winter and spring can throw at it. I'll plant every variety of hellebore I can get my hands on. Gardeners who grow hellebores universally agree that it has been falsely accused. Its scent is very faint. Very few perennials flower as long—three months or more—or under such adverse conditions. I plant them in dense shade and heavy soil where nothing else will grow. The flowers stay on the plant drying as the seedpods form in their center. They seed themselves prolifically. I used to dig the seedlings and coddle them in individual pots through the summer before moving them to permanent places in the garden in the fall. I now know that coddling is unnecessary. Even the year-old sprouts transplant easily to new locations. However, it will be three or four years before the seedlings flower.

Finally, a plant that has received a bum rap as a stinker: to many people, privet is regarded as bad news. In fact, common privet, *Ligustrum vulgare*, has white flowers with a heavy but pleasant scent. It is the California privet, *L. ovalifolium*, which grows so densely it is most often planted as a screen, that is in bad odor.

7 scented rooms

I KNOW OF NO GIFT as wonderful as a bouquet of fragrant flowers. Rayford Reddell, a friend who is a professional rose grower, for no reason sent me my most memorable bouquet of all. He claimed to have had a slow week at his California nursery, which left him with a surplus of cut garden-grown roses. Rather then let them go to waste, he overnighted me twelve dozen. Twelve dozen! A gift of roses is always welcome, but this extravagance made me giddy. I quickly organized a party for the next night. The roses set the festive mood and the guests couldn't find fault with anything. When I was asked where I had gotten the beautiful flowers, I whispered, oh so softly, that a gentleman friend had sent them. (Good gossip always enlivens a party.) What this has done for my reputation you can well imagine. And I had roses all over the house. After this floral orgy, only one question remained: How could I ever again be satisfied with less?

So far as gardens are concerned, I'm glad to say that "doing with less" is not an issue. Thank goodness, the more garden flowers you cut, the more flowers that bloom. Since I'm always bringing flowers inside, this suits me fine.

"The breath of flowers is far sweeter in the air (where it comes and goes like warbling of music) than in the hand, therefore nothing is more fit for that delight than to know what be the flowers and plants that do best perfume the air."

—FRANCIS BACON

the strength of the scent Gathering a bunch of flowers and bringing them inside is the best way to get to know them. Flowers, like people, are often very different close-up. They reveal the complexity

107

There is a story told about an elderly gardener who loved to show his garden to *visitors*. While giving a tour, he would point out the fragrant flowers. Polite guests would always bend down for a sniff. If someone mentioned they couldn't find the scent in a flower or didn't find it as wonderful as he described, he would quietly pick the flower and place it under his hat. Later, as visitors were leaving, he would remove his hat, and the flower's fragrance would be unmistakable. Encouraged by the warm, moist, confined atmosphere, the fragrance became collected and concentrated instead of being dissipated by the wind.

of their scents, and under these conditions one flower's scents can more easily be compared to another's. Often the quiet and restrained ones in the garden are only too ready to distill their perfume in the calm of a warm room.

Depending on its scent and intensity, a bloom can be an asset or a liability when added to a flower arrangement. The potency of some flowers can drown out other fragrances. With its powerful scent of tuberoses, one flower spike of bugbane *(Cimicifuga racemosa)* can mask the softer perfume of the more numerous roses, jasmine tobacco *(Nicotiana alata)* and Andean sage *(Salvia discolor)* in the same bouquet. Since I like the fragrance, I welcome its aggressiveness.

But lesser calamint *(Calamintha nepeta)* is another story. It has the misty look of baby's breath, airy and delicate, lending itself easily to flower arrangements. Its small, pale lilac flowers bloom in profusion on eighteen-inch stems all summer long thriving despite summer heat and occasional drought. The flowers retain their peppermint scent as they dry on the stems. I have gathered dried flowers in February and their scent is still strong. It remains potent when the time comes for midwinter or early-spring cleanup.

But while the fragrance of lesser calamint is subtle and agreeable in the garden, in an arrangement it will overpower other flowers with its sweet mint aroma. I suppose if we changed our centerpieces on the dining-room table to complement each course of the meal, I might welcome it as the dessert flower. Mint, however, is not one of my favorite flavors or scents, so I leave it in the garden. Planted outdoors in an herb garden or near a path, the scent can be delightfully invigorating. Unlike most herbs, it prefers a rich garden soil.

A flower's reaction to being plucked and placed in water is also a factor in the strength of its scent. The sweet fragrance of the summer hyacinth, *Galtonia candicans*, strengthens when the stem is cut and placed in water, while the nose-twisting pungency of marigolds dissipates. This is also true of

alliums. The family's signature scent of onions, carried in the stems and leaves, decreases in water. As previously noted, some real stinkers such as skunk cabbage can be housebroken by a soaking in cold water outdoors for ten minutes or so.

longer lasting flowers Although not effective as the commercial preservatives, a few drops of liquid household bleach and a teaspoon of sugar added to each quart of water can prolong blooms. The bleach prevents fungus from growing, and the sugar, a quick-energy food, feeds the flowers.

Refrigeration slows down or stops the evaporation of the essential oils of fragrant plants. Inadvertently I conducted a simple experiment demonstrating this: After picking a bunch of sweet peas one summer day, I put them overnight in the refrigerator. The next morning when I took them out and set them on the table, I couldn't detect any scent. A short time later while I was working in an adjoining room, the vase warmed, weeping drops of water. The sweet pea scent floated into my room and caressed me with its intensely sweet, piercing perfume. It was strong enough to distract me from my work. I had to bring the flowers close so I could admire their beauty along with their scent. The perfume continued drifting to me in waves throughout the day.

When arranging flowers, always remove all the foliage below the water line. If foliage rots under water the flowers decay faster, and even the best smelling aromatic foliage produces a rank odor. This is usually a pleasant chore, as aromatic leaves leave their scent on your hands.

There are a few tricks for flowers on woody stems—lilacs, witch-hazel, and other flowering shrubs. Smashing the bottom inch or two of the stem exposes more surface and allows more water to be absorbed. I smash the stems on a cutting board with a hammer. Some floral designers find that simply breaking a stem leaves it sufficiently ragged and open. Another trick is to place the recut tip of the stem in boiling water for a minute before moving it into tepid water. This forces water to flow up the stem faster.

Lilacs last longer if all their foliage is removed. Lilac foliage can be added on a separate stem for a natural look in the bouquet. Removing the leaves from the flower stem reduces the water loss through transpiration. One stem cannot support both foliage and flowers.

Roses benefit from having their stems recut every few days. I've observed that the shorter the stem, the longer they last. Some flower arrangers strip the thorns off their roses, and there are gadgets to do the job. But removing the thorns leaves wounds on the stem, and open wounds decay rather quickly underwater. Decay shortens the bloom. The overstuffed blossoms of old-fashioned roses shed their petals slowly over a few days—a wonderful way to go. I like the wanton look of fallen petals, which retain their scent until they dry.

The longevity of a cut flower differs with each individual variety. Oriental lilies are exceptionally long-lived indoors, easily lasting two weeks, if picked when the first flower on the stem opens. Since the lower flowers open first and the progression of bloom proceeds up the stem, a lily only needs you to tidy it up, removing the spent blooms, to look its best. A sweet-smelling daylily's flowers are brief but memorable. Each flower lasts a day, withering or closing in the evening, but they can be tricked into staying open at night by refrigerating them during the day. They also last without water for a day, and I often lay them on a coffee table or wear one on a straw hat.

A heavily sweet-scented datura flower lasts one night in the garden, but if plucked as soon as it opens and before it is pollinated, it will stay in bloom for several days indoors.

After waiting all summer to bloom, a tall stem of hosta 'Royal Standard' outshines its relatives by living on for weeks in water, practically to the point of needing dusting. The trumpets on the bottom open first, and as the bottom flowers are fading, the top ones open. Removing the wilted bottom flowers extends their bloom and enhances their beauty.

One summer we were leaving for vacation in the Adirondacks just as the hosta 'Royal Standard' came into bloom. Unwilling to miss the show, I traveled with a bunch rolled in newspaper and out of water for more than

eight hours. Everyone in the car enjoyed the decadence and the depth of their powerfully sweet scent. During the car ride the hosta never complained of thirst, and the bouquet lasted two weeks more in a vase in our cabin.

Tricks for lengthening the life of flowers indoors are all well and good, but I must confess to sometimes simply gathering and plopping flowers into water. Even if they don't last, it's better to have flowers for a short time than not at all.

when to harvest
Knowing the best point at which to harvest a particular flower extends its life in the vase. For the best fragrance, gather them after the dew is dried in the morning. Rose petals for making perfume are harvested before ten in the morning because by noon, 30 percent of the oil is lost to evaporation, and by four in the afternoon, 70 to 80 percent is gone.

The sooner flowers are put in water, the better. Relatively little water is absorbed through the leaves or the stems of most flowers (violets are an exception and can take in water through all parts of their body), so contrary to conventional wisdom, flowers need not soak up to their necks. The only advantage in having "six inches of water rather than one inch is that water flows six inches up the water-conducting tissues of the stem, reducing the height the water must be moved by capillary action," according to Dr. Allan Armitage in *Specialty Cut Flowers*. Any higher, and the flowers become crowded and air circulation is reduced around and between the leaves and the blossoms.

Sixty thousand *rose blossoms* are required to produce one ounce of rose oil. A hundred pounds of lavender produce three pounds of lavender oil. Understandably, essential oils are expensive.

Growers of peonies for the florist market cut them in the bud stage, condition them in water for several hours, and then store them flat in a refrigerator without water or moist air for up to four weeks. This makes it possible to stagger and extend shipments to florists. When their stems are trimmed and placed in water, the peonies act as if they were just brought in from the garden. They gradually open and bloom for a week or more.

Sweetly scented snapdragons are cut when half to two-thirds of the flowers are open; they will last for five to eight days. Stock is cut when half the flowers are open on the stem. They need to be put in water immediately and moved out of the heat of the sun. If their stems are recut frequently, the vase life is extended by three more days, from seven to ten. The pungent yarrow, if cut after the pollen is visible, stays fresh for seven to twelve days. The baby-powder-sweet garden phlox are best cut when half of the flowers on the stem are open, whereupon they will last from five to seven days. Cut the calendula for their squeaky-clean scent before the flowers open fully and bring them in as an air freshener for the kitchen table. The spicy Sweet William, *Dianthus barbatus*, is taller and better for cutting than its shorter cousins, the clove pinks. It lasts longest if cut when half of the flowers in a cluster are open.

Daffodils pose their own set of problems. They last longer if their anthers are cut off. It is best not to combine them in an arrangement with other flowers, because they secrete a slimy sap detrimental to many other varieties. Their mucilage, or sap, clogs the water-uptake channels of, for example, roses, carnations, freesias, and tulips. If they are to be arranged with other flowers, daffodils should be first left overnight in their own water or for a few hours in a bleach solution (five to seven drops of household bleach per quart of water) to allow the mucilage to run out of their stems.

Single large-flowered daffodils last longer when cut in their goose-neck stage, as their color begins to show but before the flower opens. Double-flowered daffodils are cut as the flowers begin to open. Generally they all last from four to six days in water. Stored in a refrigerator at 32 to 33 degrees they keep for ten days. Dr. Allan Armitage found that preservatives rarely enhanced the vase life of daffodils.

Tulips also prefer their water "straight up," without flower preservatives. These spunky flowers are among the thirstiest; they continue to grow taller in the vase, often an inch or more. As they do this they bend and twist toward the light, creating a charming design all their own. I don't understand why florists prefer to wire tulips into unnaturally straight postures.

It is not unusual to find the buds of peonies and hostas covered with ants when you cut them. The ants do no harm. The sweet, sticky sap at the base of the buds attracts them. When ants are present, simply dip the opening flowers upside down in a bucket of warm water for a minute or two before bringing them inside. The ants will stay in the water and the flowers will be unharmed. (If ants are creating problems by building anthills in the garden, by the way, an old-time remedy is to pour coffee on them and sprinkle the used grounds around. The ants magically disappear.)

Frequently when discarding a bouquet of flowers, I sort through them instead of throwing out the whole lot. Flowers vary in the length of time they last in water. Some, like Mexican sage and lavender, continue to look good long after other flowers in the same arrangement have wilted. They can have their stems recut and be used in another bouquet or saved as dried flowers. Both of their scents are prominent even after a year.

The colorful petals of other flowers can be collected for potpourri. Sometimes the inside petals on roses I'm about to discard are dried and spotless and can be added straight to my potpourri jar.

Harvesting flowers is a planned activity, involving a conscious attempt to cut them at the "proper" time. Spontaneity is more enjoyable. Often when walking through the garden I can't resist picking a single flower I want to get to know better. It either ends up in my buttonhole or in a bud vase over the kitchen sink. Sometimes I have a half dozen or more flowers picked on different days up there. They certainly don't add up to a sophisticated arrangement—the vases don't match nor do the flowers' colors complement each other—but it cheers me. I visit the kitchen sink more times in the day than I care to recount, and the flowers always capture my attention for a few moments. The windowsill has become my laboratory. I instinctively lift and smell a flower, often the same one, at different times of the day. This is a spur-of-the-moment activity, but doing it I realize how deeply flowers have worked their way into the pattern of my daily life. Now the row of bud vases waits patiently on the sills even when empty.

8 family portraits

FRAGRANT PLANTS CAN BE GROUPED in families for easy reference, and that is what I have done in this chapter. The most important point to remember, however, is that each plant, no matter what its birthright or its family's reputation, must be judged on its own. Scent is intensely variable, even within plant families. Species crocuses are fragrant, but their cousins the "giant" flowered Dutch hybrids are not. And of the thousands of daffodils in the market, the range of fragrances runs the gamut from scentless to powerfully sweet and on to pungent.

In this regard, it is dangerous to make assumptions or leap to conclusions. I am reminded of the time a small child pointed to a dahlia in my cutting garden and asked if he could cut the flower because he liked its smell. I was sure he must be mistaken—most dahlias are scentless—but out of the mouths of babes comes remarkable wisdom. He, of course, was closer to the ground than I, and naturally he noticed it first. It is always best to check an individual flower for scent and not jump to conclusions based on the behavior of other members of its family.

So if your dream is for a garden of fragrance, smell the flowers before you purchase the plants. When ordering plants from a catalog, never assume a plant is fragrant. Order only plants that are described as fragrant, or better yet only when their fragrances are described in detail.

The family portraits that follow are intended to be a sort of compendium of information, and in some cases duplicate material found elsewhere in this book. The families I have chosen to portray are among my favorites for a fragrant garden and have a family reputation for fragrance. Zones are given directly after the first mention of a cultivar. If no zone is given, the plant is grown as an annual.

Daphne sp., daphne
SHRUB; SUN, PART SHADE

The daphne family is not large—fifty or so members—yet mention the name and gardeners become rhapsodic singing their praises. The daphne flowers could easily go unnoticed if it were not for their fragrance, which embraces all who pass by. Once you've been captured by their scent you too will seek them out.

    Daphne odora, the fragrant daphne (Zones 7 to 9), blooms earlier than others, between late February and mid-March. Tovah Martin calls it the prototype of daphne scents. As a family, daphnes have a unique spicy scent, that she describes as "rose-touched and anise-laced." 'Aureo-marginata' is hardier than the species and is the one I grow. It fills a shady area of the perennial garden and blooms early and long with a fragrance that carries on the breeze even in cold air.

    Daphne mezereum, the February daphne (Zones 4 to 9), receives rave reviews from friends who grow it, despite the fact that it doesn't bloom in February, more likely late March and April. Its exceptional scent smells a little like honeysuckle, and it pours it out as if its sole purpose in life was to distill perfume. The four-pointed flowers can be a ghostly shade of lilac or a violet-red, but there is also a white cultivar, which I regard as special. In the fall, the species produces red berries and the white cultivar, yellow ones.

    Daphne cneorum is the rose daphne (Zones 4 to 7). It stays low to the ground, reaching only six to twelve inches, but spreads to cover two feet in all directions. In April and May the rose daphne blooms like an oriental carpet with small, delightfully fragrant rose-pink flowers. At summer's end it often flowers

again, although with fewer blooms. The named cultivars include 'Eximia', with larger flowers; 'Pygmaea', a more prostrate form; 'Ruby Glow', with darker pink flowers; and 'Variegata', with leaves delicately edged in cream.

Daphne x *burkwoodii* (Zones 4 to 8) is a taller grower, possibly reaching four feet. Its May-blooming flowers are creamy white to lightly pink. Like its parent, *Daphne caucasica* (Zones 6 to 8), it will remain evergreen or lose its leaves depending on the severity of the winter. 'Carol Mackie' is the star of this group, with variegated leaves edged in cream, an attractive shrub year-round. Although she only grows to three feet, she gets a little broad at the hips, so give her room.

I don't understand why *Daphne caucasica* isn't as well-known or as easy to buy as the other daphnes. It is a gardener's dream, blooming nine months of the year, stopping only when winter temperatures hover at freezing. Their full-out allover bloom is not shabby or scattered. Come to think of it, *D. caucasica* keeps up its appearance on its own. I have never noticed dead, unsightly flowers hanging on the bush.

Despite the cold, when I have picked flowers for the Christmas table, they have retained their fragrance. In my garden, where winters are mild, *D. caucasica* is usually evergreen; it only dropped its leaves once in six years. Unfortunately, the shrub is prone to heart attacks—I have no other explanation for its often sudden and untimely death. The shrubs are known to grow and bloom for years, seeming in the best of health, and then suddenly to die. It happens so fast that there is no retrieving them and no explanation. There is a lethal virus, however, that affects some daphnes, *D. mezereum* in particular. Consequently, to hedge my bet I plant a new *Daphne caucasica* in a different place every few years.

I grow the lilac daphne, *Daphne genkwa* (Zones 5 to 8), as a curiosity, a garden character, not a beauty. Its sharp-purple flowers cover its three-foot-high naked branches in early May. It carries little fragrance and has a reputation for being temperamental. I have only found a trace of a scent on rare occasions, but I have not found it difficult to grow.

Dianthus sp., pinks, carnations

PERENNIAL, BIANNUAL, ANNUAL; SUN

Dianthus is a large family of annuals, biennials, and perennials. Their outstanding fragrance and beautiful flowers have endeared them to gardeners for centuries. Their signature scent is spicy, yet it might be distinctly clove or nutmeg or sugarcoated with sweetness. The hardy varieties tend to have a more intense perfume.

Nicknamed pinks, not for their colors (although pink dominates) but because their fringed petals look as if cut with pinking shears, the irresistible pink is nearly as varied in form as in color. It may be flat, single, or double, or shaped like a rose. Singles and doubles alike have petals delicately or sharply fringed, feathered, lacy, pinked, or jagged in shades from pure white to light rose, and on to crimson and the hue of a glowing fire. The same flower often is blotched, penciled, or bordered with complementary or contrasting tints so that a pure white may be pricked with crimson, and a rose color streaked with a vivid red. The blossoms may even be marbled, and spotted with contrasting color zones.

Foliage colors range from light green to blue-green; the leaves are long and narrow, like blades of grass.

Sweet William, *D. barbatus* (Zones 3 to 9), has the showiest flowers. The individual single blooms are tightly packed together into large domed heads. The lighter colored flowers tend to be more strongly scented than the darker hues. Some have a light clove scent, others the freshness of baby powder. Their popularity peaked early in the seventeenth century when hardly a garden was without them. Undoubtedly, their fall from favor was led by the fact that most Sweet Williams are biennials flowering the second summer from seed. In my experience they are self-reliant, reseeding and returning each year to the same spot.

Maiden pinks, *D. deltoides* (Zones 3 to 9), seed themselves readily, even growing in cracks or out of stone walls and thriving in partial shade. Each plant forms its own mat up to three feet wide. *D. chinensis*, the China

pink, is sweet and spicy. *D. allwoodii* (Zones 4 to 8) are the old-fringed pinks crossed with the perpetual flowering carnations. Consequently, they are scarcely ever out of bloom. This habit wears them out sooner than other pinks, and they last only a few years in the garden.

I find it simpler to propagate dianthus from seed or cuttings than from divisions. Their roots are extremely compact compared to their exuberant top growth, and when dividing them often as not I find I'm cutting foliage without a piece of root attached. The whole root must be lifted before it is divided. Only then can you see where to cut.

All of the dianthus resent wet soils and are susceptible to rotting at the soil line. Experts say they prefer a sandy, alkaline soil, but I have had no problem growing them in a heavier acid soil.

Jasminum sp., jasmine
VINE; SUN, LIGHT SHADE

Jasmine is one of the most celebrated of flower fragrances, a scent used to describe other flower fragrances. It is sweet and full-bodied. Tovah Martin describes it as "tainted by a touch of fermented citrus." I don't agree. I find the fragrance of jasmine irresistible anywhere. Besides its value as a garden plant, jasmine is an ingredient in many expensive perfumes and a flavoring in tea. It is revered in the Orient, where one of its uses is for scenting temples during religious observances.

There are over two hundred species of true jasmine, but many scented look-alike plants are commonly called jasmine even though they belong to other families. The Carolina jasmine (*Gelsemium sempervirens*, Zones 7 to 10) is one of the nonjasmine jasmines. It is not always easy to tell the real from the impostors. Plants of other families often use the species name of jasminoides. There is the potato vine (*Solanum jasminoides*, Zone 10), the confederate jasmine (*Trachelospermum jasminoides*, Zones 8 to 10), and the cape jasmine (*Gardenia jasminoides* 'Prostrata,' Zones 9 to 10). Even the common names of true jasmine are confusing. Both *J. nudiflorum* (Zones 6 to 10) and *J. polyanthum* (Zones 9

to 10) are known as winter jasmine, while *J. nitidum* and *J. officinale grandiflorum* (Zones 7 to 10) are both called angel-wing jasmine, and *J. nitidum* and *J. polyanthum* share the name star jasmine. So if you're not sure which vine you're growing, you're in good company. Don't be deterred by the confusion of names. Jasmines are plants to be grown and enjoyed.

J. polyanthum blooms in winter, starting around Valentine's Day with clusters of powerfully lily-scented, starry white flowers opening from rosy pink buds. The individual flowers are small, no more than an inch across. *J. tortuosum* (Zone 9 to 10), a South African jasmine, possesses a fruity scent. *J. humile* 'Revolutum' (Zone 7 to 10) is a yellow-flowered Asian variety with the spicy scent of carnations. *J. molle* (Zone 7 to 10) is from Australia and has a powerful scent of citrus with the sweetness of gardenia.

J. nitidum (Zones 9 to 10) answers to many names: angel-wing jasmine, star jasmine, windmill jasmine, and royal jasmine are the ones most used. But by whatever name it is unforgettable. This jasmine requires a long, warm growing period to bloom. Where temperatures go below 25 degrees Fahrenheit, it is not reliable when young. As it ages it can tolerate colder weather. Given the conditions it likes, it quickly becomes a small bush smothered in white flowers. It makes a good container plant or a chubby ground cover blooming nearly year-round. Tovah Martin describes its scent as boasting "a squeaky-clean, soapy scent like fresh laundry aired on a spring day."

The jasmine famed as an ingredient in French perfume is *J. officinale grandiflorum* (Zones 9 to 10), a double, sweetly scented white jasmine whose fragrance is strong in the evening. Its glossy leaves and heavily sweet-scented, pink-tinted buds open into two-inch white pinwheels.

Hybrids of *J. sambac* (Zones 9 to 10) are the most popular for growing as houseplants, because they're happiest at temperatures above 60 degrees. 'Maid of Orleans' has semidouble flowers that bloom off and on throughout the year and possess a hauntingly spicy scent. Well-mannered, it lets you know when it is about to cease blooming, because its white flowers then blush to wine red. *J.s. flore-pleno* 'Grand Duke of Tuscany' is a double, with flowers resembling miniature roses.

Most jasmines are not prima donnas and are easily grown indoors in a pot. They don't even pine for lack of high humidity, and will set spicy buds on an east- or west-facing window. Many, like the hybrids of *J. sambac*, thrive at household temperatures of 60 degrees and above.

Each family has its black sheep, and *J. nudiflorum* (Zone 6 to 10) and *J. mesnyi* (Zones 8 to 9) are the nonperformers among the jasmines. Both have scentless yellow flowers.

Jasmine takes pride in its personal appearance, and the flowers fall before they brown or discolor, so a vine always looks good. I often gather the still fresh and fragrant fallen blooms and scatter them on the dinner table as decorations.

Lathyrus odorata, sweet peas
ANNUAL VINE; SUN

The sweet peas, *Lathyrus odoratus*, are the first ladies of scented annuals. Their scent has the depth and complexity of orange blossoms with a pinch of vanilla, a twist of old rose, and an intoxicating honey sweetness. The fragrance is so cunning that sweet peas never reveal their makeup all at once. They tease us and leave us wanting more.

Each delicate, airy flower is shaped like a miniature sunbonnet. At the height of bloom, the ruffled blossoms cover the graceful, curving vines. They flower on side shoots off the central stem, so they are easy to cut for arrangements without shortening the vine or depleting its beauty in the garden. I've cut every flower off a vine one day only to return and pick another handful the next.

Unfortunately, sweet peas have slid into oblivion since they had their moment of glory a hundred years ago. And yet, once someone sees them, it is love all over again. I've been growing them annually for seven years, and each spring as the time comes to set my seedlings out into the garden, the phone rings with requests from friends asking if I could spare a few. Anticipating the demand this year, I've started over a hundred pots so that I will have plenty to plant—and to share.

How did these sweet-smelling charmers ever lose their place in the sun? Perhaps their reputation was damaged by rumors of temperamental behavior and short bloom. It's true they can be slow to germinate, but they aren't difficult to grow. Still, sweet peas are rarely seen among the popular flats sold at local garden centers, and how many of us have the patience to grow plants from seed anymore? But I promise that once you grow these enchanting flowers, you'll want to grow them every year.

In the southernmost states, sweet-pea seeds are sown outdoors around the end of October to bloom through the mild winter into the spring. Further north, where winter's snow doesn't stay too long or freeze too deeply, plant in late November or early December. Early bloomers could start to flower by mid-May; most wait until June.

I could plant seeds as soon as the frost is out of the ground and the soil is dry, but I find I get stronger plants and a longer bloom if I start the seeds indoors in late January and move the seedlings outside with some protection in late March. For good germination, soak the seeds for four hours, more or less. (I have unintentionally left them soaking for several days with no ill effects.) Plant them in a sterile growing medium.

If you get a late start, the seeds can be speeded up by being grown under lights twenty-four hours a day. They don't need any rest or darkness. However, the soil will dry out and need water several times a day. This requires a constant vigil. If they are allowed to dry out even for a short time they are weakened and die.

Since the seedlings resent transplanting, I start them in well-labeled three-inch peat pots that can be planted directly into the soil. If you plan to start seeds indoors, plant them in a moistened (but not soggy) sterile growing medium, cover them with an inch of soil, and place the pots under grow lights or in a sunny window. Check the soil daily; don't allow it to dry out. Snip tops now and then to promote branching.

Martha Kraska, renowned in our part of the country for her sweet peas, credits her cat for her early success. The first year she grew them, her cat ate the tops off a tray of three-inch-tall seedlings. She noticed that they

began to come back quickly, branching as they grew. Now, each winter she keeps the cat away and snips the top of the young sweet peas herself several times during their early growth so they fill out well.

Before you move the seedlings outdoors, you must harden them off. By day, place them outdoors in a protected place—a cold frame or next to the house. Bring them in at night. (When I have lots of plants, I keep them on a wheelbarrow and wheel it into the garage at night.) After several days of adjusting, the plants can be left out overnight to finish the process. For extra protection, a garden blanket, a thin synthetic cover sold by nurseries and some garden centers, will hold moisture, let in light, and keep plants warm. After a few more days, you can plant them in their permanent spots in the garden.

To increase their length of bloom, sweet peas need deep roots, which stay cool and moist in the hot sun. I first dig a trench two feet deep, in which I place a mix of compost, well-rotted manure and topsoil. A sprinkling of lime is also appreciated.

Before I set the seedling out, I cut a few slits in the peat pot to aid the roots in breaking out of the pot and growing into the soil. I place the pot in the trench with the top several inches below the ground; I then bury the pot and up to an inch of the stem. As the plant gets taller, I hoe soil on the sides to keep it upright, eventually completely filling the trench and burying several inches of the stem. Consequently the original roots are planted deeper and the buried stem may sprout more roots.

If you're sowing seeds directly into the garden, fill the trench to within six inches of the top and plant seeds two inches deep and three to four inches apart. Water them in well to get them off to a good start and never let them lack for water as they grow. Sweet peas can be as demanding of rich food and long, cool drinks as roses. A trench will collect and hold water, as well as protect young seedlings from damaging wind and severe cold. Later, your seedlings can be thinned out and spaced from nine to twelve inches apart.

A few inches of mulch, even a flat stone placed next to the stems, helps to keep the roots cool and prolong bloom. Last year, the sweet peas that crowded into the back of the flower borders where their bottoms were shaded

by the surrounding flowers bloomed longer than the vines more generously spaced in the cutting garden.

While there are bush types, most sweet peas are climbing vines with tendrils that grab and twist around supports like a corkscrew. The description by Keats comes to mind: "Here are sweet peas, on tiptoe for a flight: with wings of gentle flush o'er delicate white, and taper fingers catching at all things to bind them all about with tiny rings."

Plant sweet peas where they can climb on a fence, a trellis, or the side of a building. If you have a picket fence, the tendrils won't be able to get around the wide boards, so drape the fence with black plastic netting, which is nearly invisible and gives the tendrils a leg up. Seedlings need support as soon as the tendrils appear, when plants are tall enough to lean.

Blooms start after three months of strong growth, for which temperatures of 50 to 60 degrees are ideal. Cutting blooms for bouquets and deadheading those left on the vine is crucial. With attentive pruning, sweet peas will continue to flower for three months or longer. But if you stop cutting the flowers, be warned: The plants will go to seed with lightning speed.

I grow a half dozen varieties of sweet peas in pots on the terrace where we frequently dine. A sixteen-inch pot supports three vines twining about a tepee of bamboo poles. The base of the pots are kept shaded by other taller potted plants and furniture, while the vines grow up into the sunlight. I also planted a few vines to grow through large shrubs: Rambling through a purple-leaved smoke bush, fragrant pink sweet peas are a breathtaking sight, and reason enough for a revival!

I was surprised to learn how many of the cultivars I grow were popular at the turn of the century. 'Eckford's Finest Mix' was bred in 1898 by Henry Eckford, the premier sweet-pea breeder in England. 'Black Knight', also bred by him, is listed as one of the best sweet peas of 1910. The maroon, almost black flowers are a knockout. 'Captain of the Blues', an 1890 Eckford introduction, sets the standard for bright purple-blue flowers. 'Mars', from 1895, has large frilly, cream-white flowers flecked and striped with ruby red. Two of the newer varieties I like are the color mixes of 'Floral Tribute' and 'Fragrantissima'.

A Garden of Fragrance

Lilium sp., lilies

BULBS; SUN, PART SHADE; ZONES 3 TO 10

"The time has come for lilies to take their rightful place in rank next to the rose. The rose is still the reigning sovereign and requires much more pampering than the humble Cinderella-like lily, which has only recently left the ashes of neglect to come to court." So said Helen Morgenthau Fox in *Garden Cinderellas*, written in 1928. Her advice seems to have been taken; lilies are indeed easy to grow and more popular now than ever before.

The lily and its descendants through the ages have played a role in history that has merged into legend. Ancient Greeks and Romans thought of the lily as the flower of love, the centerpiece of ceremonies in the worship of Aphrodite and Venus. Through countless ages the lily has been the symbol of purity and chastity, linked to the Madonna herself. The reverence for the *Lilium candidum* ("candidum" means "dazzling white") is responsible for its being named the Madonna lily. To the Turks, the lily was food, and they roasted bulbs to a turn under hot embers.

Lilium encompasses a large group of bulbs indigenous to the northern temperate regions of both hemispheres, although the largest number originate in eastern Asia. The sizes of their bulbs vary from *L. tenuifolium*, not much bigger than a marble, to *L. giganteum*, the size of a softball. Accordingly, their heights range from the fifteen-inch *L. rubellum* to the ten- to twelve-foot *L. giganteum*. Individual flowers may turn up or nod down in bowl or trumpet shapes. Some face down with petals curving up like flaps upon a winter hat.

The lily scent is distinctive, and other scents are often compared to it. Still, as with other fragrant families, there is no single lily scent. The Turk's cap–shaped flowers of *L. kelloggii*, an American native found from northwest California to southwest Oregon, "emits a soft honey-like scent"; *L. candidum* has been compared to "heather honey"; *L. longiflorum* is reminiscent of "a gentle jasmine-like perfume"; *L. regale* has a rich "honeysuckle perfume"; the Ambrosia lily mixture sold by White Flower Farm is said to have a "freesia-like" fragrance, while the American Classic series marketed by Wayside Gardens is simply "spicy." Most of the time a lily fragrance is eulogized as "delightful," "wonderful," "rich," "sweetly penetrating," and "intoxicating." But beware—among the perfumed progeny of this ever-expanding family there are also scentless siblings.

It used to be that scarlet or orange lilies carried little or no scent. Since Asiatic lilies were born scentless, the Oriental lilies cornered the perfume market. But in the last ten years, crosses have been perfected between the Easter lily *(L. longiflorum)* and Asiatic lilies. One series, the Ambrosia lilies, features a mixture of lightly scented flowers in soft shades from cream to lavender. While they don't compare with the Orientals for intensity of fragrance, I applaud the progress toward adding scents. Lily breeders are plainly headed down the right road.

The martagon lily *(L. martagon)* is pollinated by moths and consequently is strongly perfumed at night. ("Martagon" comes from the Turkish word for a kind of turban, and is used to describe the Turk's-cap lilies. Nodding flowers with reflexed petals are often called martagon-shaped.)

The Oriental lilies are the most flamboyant family members and have forceful personalities, generally featuring large blooms and great beauty. Two well-known and long-grown Oriental lilies, hard to surpass for their beauty and scent, are 'Casa Blanca' and 'Star Gazer.' Another Oriental, the Easter lily is parent to a number of classic trumpet-shaped flowers in different shades. 'Amethyst Temple' and the Golden Sunburst Strain are both well named.

L. auratum, the gold band lily of Japan, known for its large fragrant flowers, was an early import to the United States and was growing here in the 1860s. A cultivar called 'Gold Band' attains a height of only three feet. Its flowers have an irresistible face, gold-streaked white freckled with crimson. Thirty or more blossoms on a stem are not unusual. In a summer when weather is tame and the wind submissive, blooms continue for eight weeks. *L. auratum* has been considerably used for breeding and the offspring vary greatly.

All the hybridizing being done between lilies complicates keeping them straight. The so-called American Classics series of tetraploid, hybrid

Chinese trumpet lilies carry the names of national parks—'Yellowstone', 'Yosemite', 'Grand Teton', and so forth. Does this make them American? Are they naturalized citizens? If their fragrance lives up to its promise, I certainly hope so. Breeders have created fragrant dwarf oriental lilies such as the 'Little Rascal' series. A cross between the Easter lily and Asiatic hybrids yielded the 'Fragrant ShowTime' lily series. Each year the catalogs bring new lily crosses and introductions.

L. formosanum is the last lily to bloom but worth the wait.

September and October are better for its presence. Rising between six and eight feet and wafting a strong sweet scent, it dominates the other flowers.

There was a time when lilies were thought to be difficult to grow and gardeners were wary of trying. In fact, the bulbs were often underfed and mistreated in shipping, so many harbored disease. Growers and shippers now understand the problems and the best lilies coming to market are grown from seed. If you purchase bulbs from a reliable source and don't leave them sitting in water, most will be easy and accommodating, blooming for many years.

When picking lilies for arrangements, cut as little of the stem as needed. The lily depends on its leaves and stems to nurture the bulb as it forms next year's flower. (Be aware: the pollen of lilies is easily rubbed or shaken off the flowers and may stain clothing. Florists regularly clip off the stamens to prevent such problems.)

Narcissus sp., daffodils
BULBS; SUN, PART SHADE; ZONES 4 TO 10
(EXCEPT TAZETTA TYPES, ZONES 8 TO 10)

Daffodils have been cultivated for hundreds of years and are the essence and breath of spring. Daffodil is the common name for all *Narcissus* sp., and jonquil is the common name for the very fragrant small group of *N. jonquilla* and its cultivars and hybrids. Daffodil genealogy is a confusing tangle of species and naturally occurring hybrids. Some experts list up to seventy species, while others group some as subspecies. The Royal Horticultural Society and the Ameri-

can Daffodil Society have established the most widely used and practical classifications. They recognize eleven divisions of daffodils. Those in Divisions I through IV and the cyclamineus hybrids do not produce much perfume, although there are exceptions such as the musk-scented 'Louise de Coligny', 'Abba', and 'Sweet Charity'. Division V, the triandrus daffodils, possess a fruity scent. Division VI, the cyclamineus, are known for their flared-back petals, not their scent. But 'Jenny' is a favorite of mine. I love her more for her looks, those swept-back locks of pure white petals, than her sweetly medicinal scent. Division VII includes the jonquilla hybrids and is the group with the most scented members. The tazetta daffodils, Division VIII, are known for their strong musky scent, while the poeticus, Division IX, tend toward a strong spicy scent. The wild and species forms grouped in Division X are mostly scented. The showy division XI split-corona daffodils are a mixed bag of scented and scentless.

In general, the daffodils with the most penetrating fragrance are near relatives of *N. jonquilla*, *N. tazetta*, and *N. poeticus.* Of the thousands of named cultivars on the market, those related to *jonquilla*, a small-flowered species, are the ones most cultivated for their fragrance. 'Baby Moon', 'Suzy', and 'Trevithian' are some of the best of this division. These golden flowers have naturalized in the fields throughout Europe, although they originated in Spain and Portugal. Each stem has up to six flowers waving at the top. The double form is known as Queen Anne's double jonquil.

The scent of daffodils tends toward the fruity, sweet, or musk-scented, but there are also unique scents. The hoop skirt daffodil is lightly, sweetly scented. 'Tahiti' and 'Tête-à-Tête' both remind me of the scent of gardenias. In 'Unique' I find only sweetness. 'Big Gun' is cotton candy–sweet, while 'Gigantic Star' is vanilla-scented. 'Erlicheer', a tazetta type with multiple heads, is sweet-scented with an intensity all its own. 'Geranium', 'Sweetness', and 'Act' are all well-perfumed hybrids. Miniatures with a sweet scent include *N. assoanus*, 'Nylon', 'Pencrebar', and 'Hawera'.

I must caution you that all the varieties sold as 'King Alfred' I've smelled are scentless. Never trust the bulbs to be the same from year to year. Breeders know this name sells daffodils, so they substitute, mixing in similar-looking bulbs. I haven't planted it for years. There are so many more beautiful and fragrant choices.

Most of the pink daffodils tend to be scentless or very slightly fragrant. 'Fragrant Pink' is an exception. It is not an outstanding pink daffodil, but is highly perfumed. Its scent is typical of a daffodil, but has been compared to the fragrance of the rose 'Tropicana'.

Paperwhites are the daffodils most forced by florists and gardeners alike. They are rarely seen in a garden. I purchase a bundle each fall to force over the winter. Every few weeks I start a new batch.

I recommend three tazetta for forcing: 'Grand Soleil d'Or' blooms in five plus weeks. 'Galilee' is quicker, blooming in three weeks with large trusses of pure white flowers on as many as four stems. 'Chinese Sacred Lily' takes three to four weeks. A fourth favorite is 'Ziva', the longest to bloom, taking four to five weeks before its yellow flowers appear. When price shopping for bulbs, compare size as well as price. The larger sizes have more flowers.

Paeonia sp., peonies
PERENNIAL; SUN, PART SHADE; ZONES 2 TO 8

Plant a peony and no matter what your age, it will outlive you. Pass a division along to your children, and it may well become a family heirloom, going on to their children in turn.

Unfortunately, the highest compliment a fragrant peony generally receives about its smell is that it has a "coarse rose scent." Some are pleasant enough at first whiff but a rank after-breath often follows. Descendants of *Paeonia officinalis*, the common peony, usually have a rather unpleasant smell. One theory is that the petals are only lightly scented, while the pollen holds a strong rank odor. Fortunately, a peony holds its fragrance close, whatever it may be, so if you avoid putting your nose in it you'll never know any unpleasantness and can admire its beauty.

At the end of the eighteenth century, *P. lactiflora* was discovered in Siberia and it is through her arrival in Europe and subsequent marriages that

fragrance was bred into peonies. Mary Anne Metz, a horticulturist for seventeen years at Klehm's Nursery, has grown over 450 different herbaceous peonies. She has kept extensive field notes on their fragrances. As she explains, "Peony fragrances range from unpleasant to flat, to musk, sweet musk, and on to musky as in an old basement, close to moldy." The flat fragrances are ones that don't excite her. They are neither sweet nor bitter. They are just there. She further clarified her descriptions by explaining that the scent of the same peonies may vary in different years and also at different times of the day. Her favorite is 'Norma Volz', a white double, scented like lily-of-the-valley. It is an American Peony Society gold medal winner.

Wayne Winterrowd prefers the great old-fashioned doubles in peonies such as 'Sarah Bernhardt', 'Duchesse de Nemours', and 'Festiva Maxima'. He finds them cold-cream scented.

As breeders continue to hybridize peonies, their range of colors continues to expand from stark to creamy white and on to porcelain pink, hot coral, delectable raspberry, sunshine yellow, coppery salmon, burnt amber, and reds that run the gamut from chocolate-tinted to a red flame that appears to throw sparks. Many modern hybrids are even delicately tinted, combining more than one color.

And it seems that color in peonies has a mysterious association with perfume. Alice Harding, in her delightful book *The Peony*, states that double rose pink peonies are the most fragrant, while the single or semidouble reds are inclined to smell bad, and in most instances, double reds lack odor entirely.

Although all this continues to change as breeders expand the size and look of peonies—which were originally single—so that now a peony can masquerade as an oversized rose, camellia, water lily, anemone, or poppy. Petals of today's peonies may be crinkled, recurled, and frilled, narrow or broad, and arranged in flower shapes varying from bombs to bowls to salad plates. The breeders label and sell peonies as single, semidouble, double, Japanese, and bomb types. Both singles and semidoubles have golden pompons of stamens in the centers. The semidoubles differ from singles in that they have two rows of petals. The Japanese peonies resemble singles, with their flat

open flowers, but the stamen has developed into a longer and wider frill, often curled like confetti and just as showy. Doubles look like open roses, while bombs are rounder with recurring petals at their base.

The seven old-fashioned classic peonies I planted in my lilac and peony walk that were on the recommended list for commercial cut-flower production include 'Le Cygne' (ca. 1907), 'Martha Bulloch' (ca. 1907), 'Mons. Jules Elie' (ca. 1880), 'Sarah Bernhardt' (ca. 1906), 'Therese' (ca. 1904), 'Baroness Schroeder' (ca. 1889) and 'Festiva Maxima' (ca. 1851). 'Le Cygne' is famous for its beautiful form; the petals are uniquely arranged like feathers on a swan's wing. 'Martha Bulloch', a late bloomer, has a deep rose pink center and outer petals of a softer shell pink. 'Mons. Jules Elie' is the most widely grown pink double of the twentieth century; its deep pink petals are sprinkled with silver dust, and it blooms early. 'Sarah Bernhardt', another double, is seashell pink with a few center petals edged in dark rose; it blooms late. 'Therese' has double, glossy soft pink petals and blooms in midseason. Both 'Baroness Schroeder' and 'Festiva Maxima' have double white flowers and are described in more detail on page 25.

Over the years, as other fragrant peonies wafted under my nose, I added 'Cora Stubbs', 'Pink Hawaiian Coral', 'Nellie Saylor', 'Jessie', 'Cheddar Elite', and 'Raspberry Sundae'.

TREE PEONIES
SHRUB; SUN, PART SHADE

Tree peonies, mostly derivatives of *P. suffruticosa*, are among the most beautiful of all flowers. They have much in common with herbaceous peonies, but unlike their cousins do not die back to the ground in the winter, instead retaining their woody stems. This structural difference is the easiest way to tell them apart. These shrubs slowly grow to be almost as fat as they are tall, ultimately reaching four feet. In England I have seen older shrubs, of half a century or more, seven feet tall.

The flowers of a tree peony bloom earlier than those of the herbaceous varieties. Individual flowers are usually larger, some the size of six-inch

salad plates, and may be single or double. Their petals can be crinkled like crepe paper or silken and translucent with the look of fine porcelain. Often their centers have frills of golden anthers.

Tree peonies don't have a wide range of fragrances. Breeders classify two distinct scents—the lemon scent found in *P. Lutea* and the sweet and yeasty musk scent of *P. suffruticosa*. Most tree peonies smell of musk—not sweet, but not unpleasant. Occasionally, one has a spicy scent. Mary Anne Metz has not found any strong fragrances in tree peonies to date and has noticed no difference in the strength of the perfume among singles, doubles, or hybrids. Three *P. suffruticosa* sister seedlings, 'The Captain's Concubine', 'Guardian of the Monastery', and 'Companion of Serenity', all share variations of the same soft sweet scent. Normally tree peonies don't strut their stuff in containers, but 'Guardian of the Monastery' has been known to have flowers ten inches across all the while confined in a container in the corner of the greenhouse. Other tree peonies Metz recommends for their fragrances are 'Aurora', 'Hephestos', 'Hestia', 'Icarus', and 'Nike'.

Pelargonium sp., scented geraniums
HOUSEPLANT, HERBS; SUN, PART SHADE

Scented geraniums lack distinctive identity. They play floral charades, masquerading behind such borrowed scents such as those of roses, fruits, and spices.

The rose scent in geraniums is purer than that in roses and is also distilled for perfume. The reason it is so pure is that the scent is in the leaves, and where the perfume of most flowers decreases as they dry, that in leaves gets stronger. With these plants the floral sport of hybridizing was carried to extremes at the turn of the century. New introductions continue unabated, even bringing us the unlikely scents of chocolate and champagne. Recently I counted fifty-one different varieties of scented geranium in the Logee's Greenhouse mail-order catalog alone. And they sell other varieties they haven't yet listed. (It is Logee's that is credited with reviving the popularity of scented geraniums and identifying and categorizing each scent.)

One thing should be understood right away. Scented geraniums are not "plain Janes." They have a ton of soul and a dash of style. Each plant could be grown for the beauty of its stylish foliage alone. Scented geranium leaves are almost as diverse as their fragrances. They may be crimped, ruffled, or curled, deeply cut or broad, velvety or rough-hewn, deep to light green, lime, chartreuse, even splashed or penciled with gold, silver, or cream. Gertrude Jekyll described the velvety leaves of *Pelargonium tomentosum* as being "as thick as a fairy's blanket." Their various foliages are beautiful for cutting and using in arrangements or floating alone in a bowl, especially in winter when garden greens are limited. Their leaves, even when picked and dried, hold their fragrance. Consequently, crushed and dried, they are a frequent ingredient in potpourri and sleep pillows. Even a few leaves placed under a pillow reputedly induce sleep.

Before you rush out to buy a few plants (one would never be enough), it is necessary to clarify what a scented geranium is. "Geranium" is one of the most confusing of names. It is a catchall common name covering a multitude of flowers, while at the same time serving as the Latin name for a group of plants. Scented "geraniums" are in fact *Pelargoniums*. (True *Geraniums* are perennial woodland plants with small flowers that bloom in the spring.) Not all *Pelargoniums* are, of course, scented. The zonal pelargoniums, *P. hortorum*, have leaves carrying an acidic odor likened to chlorine, while the ivy geranium, *P. peltatum*, and many common geraniums, are scentless.

Among my favorite scented geraniums are 'Snowflake', with its pale green, velvet-soft leaves edged with snow. It is attractive enough to be worth growing for its foliage alone, although its leaves are saturated with a rose fragrance. 'Lemon Crispum' *(P. crispum)* has a strong lemon scent in its tiny crinkled golden leaves, each with a pyramidal shape. I suggest floating them in a finger bowl. 'Nutmeg' *(P. fragrans)* is popular for the spicy aroma of its grayish leaves. 'Strawberry' was a popular hybrid in Victorian times, when it imparted a fresh strawberry scent to toiletries.

Obviously, with hundreds of scented cultivars in the market I could continue with example after example. But then I might spoil your fun in

sniffing out your own favorites. Although the largest selection is from mail-order catalogs, scented geraniums are creeping back onto shelves wherever houseplants are sold.

When you get your chosen plants home, you'll discover them to be among the most carefree and easygoing of houseplants. As natives of South Africa, they ask only to be given a sunny window and some water when their soil is dry to the touch. Excess water or prolonged droughts are their only enemies. Insects rarely bother them. A weak liquid fertilizer is welcome monthly in spring and in summer. However, too much fertilizer reduces their scent. Some cultivars have cascading stems, making them perfect for hanging baskets, while others require a timely nip and tuck as they tend to grow leggy, tall, and spindly. A quick pinch back to broaden their hips not only keeps them full-figured but provides the leaves for potpourri, flower arrangements, or cuttings from which to grow more plants. Adventurous cooks have used the leaves for flavoring cakes, jellies, ice cream, and tea. Lovers have been known to tuck a leaf in an envelope to scent a letter.

Not having a parlor, I prefer a sunny kitchen window for growing my scented geraniums. It is easier to keep an eye on them, and they prove very useful in getting rid of unpleasant odors from cooking. After peeling onions, I rub a leaf, and instead of smelling of onions I carry their pleasant fragrance with me.

Well looked after, a scented geranium plant will last for years, the subtle influence of its fragrance and the beauty of its foliage adding charm to any room.

Rosa sp., roses
SHRUB; SUN

Perhaps the popularity of roses is due to their sensuous appeal. Roses have been steeped in history, intrigue, and romance, as well as scandal, since gardening began.

Roses, especially red roses, symbolize love. In a marvel of theatrical staging, Cleopatra surrounded her bed with several feet of rose petals when entertaining Anthony. The emperor Nero spent the equivalent of $160,000 in today's dollars on rose petals for a single sumptuous banquet, carpeting the floor with them and showering them on banquet guests from the balcony. When he visited the seashore at Naples, he demanded that it be strewn with rose petals.

Nor has the association with roses and romance died out. A modern-day Romeo, Edgar Bronfman, Jr., wooed Clarissa Alcock with long-stemmed red roses—no less than 12,480 of them in a single year. Four dozen arrived every day the two were apart.

The charm, beauty, and scent of roses have made them the most popular flowers in the world. Gerard wrote in his *Herbal* of 1636 that "the rose doth deserve the chiefest and most principall place among all floures whatsoever, beeing not onely esteemed for his beautie, vertues, and his fragrant and odorisroue smell." Fragrance, we'd like to think, is the rightful heritage of every rose. In fact, it isn't so. While many roses are indeed well known for their fragrances, plenty of the most popular best-sellers have little or no fragrance at all. 'Betty Prior', 'Simplicity', and 'The Fairy' are all scentless or only slightly scented. (I have read, incidentally, that 'Betty Prior' has a rich spicy scent, yet I have never detected any scent in the six bushes I have grown for more than a decade.)

Roses have complex ancestry and history. Their perfumes are extremely various, being compared to anise, fruits, herbs, honey, licorice, medicine, myrrh, nasturtiums, spices, tea, and violets. If the scent of a rose is evasive or difficult to pin down, it is often simply described as sweet.

Neville F. Miller's study reported in *The American Rose Journal* in 1962 (see page xvi) suggested that a relationship exists between color and scent. Red and pink roses, he found, carry the elemental rose odor, while white and yellow tend to be restricted to the elemental odors of nasturtium, tea, violet, and lemon. Orange blends carried the scent of fruit, tea, violet, nasturtium, and clove. The pinks and red roses are the most highly scented, while white and yellow roses are rarely fragrant. But exceptions to these rules abound.

For comparison's sake, fruity fragrances are used to describe many roses. 'Madame Isaac Pereire', often described as one of the most fragrant roses, has a raspberry scent, as do 'Honorine de Brabant', 'Hawaii', and 'Cerise Bouquet'. 'Gold Medal', 'New Dawn', and 'Nymphenburg' could be compared to apple, and 'Buff Beauty' to a pineapple-banana combination. Many of the new English roses have a myrrh fragrance: 'Constance Spry', 'Wife of Bath', and 'Fair Bianca'.

One of the best ways to enjoy the old-rose scent described on page 34 is to grow 'Madame Hardy', a white damask rose that blooms only once a season, but does so then with reckless abandon. In a three- or four-week period this rose produces as many flowers as a hybrid tea rose will bear over a long summer. Each individual blossom has so many petals, tucked into a cup shape, that they must stand straight up, flattened against each other. Around the flower's edges the petals appear scalloped, dividing it into quarters, and the whole ensemble is stitched together with a green button eye. Perhaps because of the abundance of petals and flowers, 'Madame Hardy' offers one of the most heady old-rose scents, noticeable several yards from the bush or beyond an open window. Strangely, the sepals of this rose have the odor of marigold.

The tea fragrance, while noted by all the experts, is controversial. Many rosarians argue that it is reminiscent of the small chests of tea shipped from the Orient to Europe. Others claim that the early roses came on boats carrying tea so the fragrance was called tea-scented by association. Peter Beales, widely recognized as an authority on old roses, writes in his book *Classic Roses* that he has yet to detect any real resemblance to the scent of tea in any of the roses. Be that as it may, there is a distinct scent—which to me smells sweet with a light pungent punch—categorized as a "tea fragrance" by some rosarians and as an orris scent by others. (Orris is extracted from the dried rhizomes of *Iris florentina*.) To learn to distinguish between them, you'll have to smell a lot of roses.

Since the scent of most roses is mainly in their petals, it follows that the double roses are more fragrant, although the quantity and quality of the

scent differs greatly from rose to rose. The double roses are likely to retain their fragrance longer, since the overlapping petals impede evaporation. Botanists assume that the production of essential oils slows down after the rose has been pollinated.

Rose petals are the main ingredient in potpourri because they hold their strong colors, not their perfume, as they dry. Only the 'Apothecary's Rose' is known to hold its fragrance after drying. The fragrance in potpourri comes from drops of essential oils added as necessary to refresh the petals' scent.

However, the fragrance of a rose is not always in the flower. The musk roses carry musk fragrance in their styles, which grow together into a column. It is surmised that their scent travels further because it is easier for air to surround and pick up the perfume from this column than to reach the base of a petal. The eglantine rose's balsamlike scent is locked in glands in the hairs on the foliage. Its scent is released naturally after a light frost or shower and can then be readily noticed. Moss roses hold their scent in the green mosslike growth at the base of each bud. This "moss" holds a sticky sap in glands at the tips of its bristles and has an air freshener fragrance of its own, similar to balsam or pine. If you touch the sap, its pleasant perfume will stay with you.

Not all roses have a pleasant fragrance. The wet leaves of *Rosa xanthina* and *R. ecae* have a rather nauseating odor, which to some writers smells like an anthill or formic acid. 'Sunsprite' and a number of other yellow roses have a licorice fragrance, placing them in the "Love-'em-or-Hate-'em" class. The *R. foedita* progeny, 'Persian Yellow', 'Austrian Yellow', and 'Austrian Copper', have been described as smelling like linseed oil.

As if this were not complicated enough, the same variety of rose planted in two different places will have similar—but not necessarily the same—scents. In addition, the perfume of some roses changes as they open and age. The rose's fragrance is in the essential oil, and an essential oil is composed of a combination of compounds. Compounds differ in vapor pressures, causing the more volatile compounds to evaporate more quickly than the others, thus altering the rose's scent. For example, when 'Crimson Glory'

137

Family Portraits

first opens it has a floral fragrance, while an older rose on the same plant that has been open for a while will have a spicy smell like cloves. 'Peace', one of the most popular roses, opens with almost no fragrance but after a few days has a pungent, spicy scent similar to that of a nasturtium.

The old-rose fragrance originated with the damask roses and is found today in 'Fashion', 'Gertrude Jekyll', 'Mary Rose', 'Penelope', 'The Reeve', 'Othello', and 'The Squire', among others. A bowl of damasks, gallicas, or noisettes will bring the best of the rose floral fragrance indoors. Even one exquisitely perfumed rose such as 'Don Juan' in a slim vase can scent a room. Picked before ten in the morning and brought into the house, roses will be more fragrant. Their perfume has not been carried off by the wind or evaporated in the heat of the sun.

A cool, moist day is best for harvesting roses whose essential oil will be distilled into attar of roses. Evaporation is slowed, and the moisture encourages the roses to produce more oil. They must be picked at the first light of dawn, because by noon, 30 percent of the oil is lost to evaporation, and by four in the afternoon, 70 to 80 percent. Commercial picking is usually complete before ten in the morning and distillation begins immediately.

Approximately once a week the rosebushes should have their spent blossoms removed. I do it less often, but I make a point of collecting the soft rose petals. This serves two purposes: the dead-heading produces more roses, and the unblemished petals can be dried or used fresh. Even though you find the blossoms wilted, the inside petals are usually perfect and the fragrance remains. They will retain their color and fragrance longer if they are protected from direct sun and humidity. If you do practice this weekly, the petals can be saved over the course of the summer for a multiplicity of little luxuries. Throw rose petals instead of rice at weddings, float rose petals in a bath to add fragrance and beauty "à la Cleopatra," steep rose petals in boiling water to make rose water, and use them to scent your dresser drawers, closets, or rooms. You may even candy rose petals to decorate cakes or desserts.

Salvia sp., sage

HERB; PERENNIAL, ANNUAL; SUN, PART SHADE

This star-studded genus of the mint family has some nine hundred species but is mostly ignored. Aside from the common cooking herb *Salvia officinalis* (Zone 8 to 10) and the ubiquitous red ornamental sage *Salvia splendens* (Zone 9 to 10), the sage family hasn't been properly introduced to home gardeners. Yet every new member I meet is better than the one before. I find myself asking, "Where have you been all my life?"

Sages' family resemblance is in their tall skinny floral spikes covered with tubular flowers, some hooked at the end and others divided like a lobster's claw. Their colors range from fiery reds, sky blues, perky pinks, and sunny yellows to snow whites and almost black. Their aromas vary from scentless to fruity and medicinal, tottering downhill toward rank.

The Andean sage, *Salvia discolor* (Zone 9 to 10), is exceptional. The stems are covered with downy white hairs, giving the stems and grayish leaves a silvery glimmer. The foliage is citrus-scented. The nearly black flowers contrast sharply with their woolly white calyces. The plant is so good-looking that I dug one up to winter over in the greenhouse where it gratefully continued blooming and growing without attracting any of the usual houseplant pests and diseases.

S. vanhouttii (Zone 9 to 10) is another stunning plant with fruit-scented foliage. It is also unique for its burgundy-colored flowers and the length of time it holds its large round buds before allowing them to open. It would be worth growing even if the buds never opened.

S. azurea pitcheri (Zone 8 to 10) is loved for the brightness and clarity of its azure-blue flowers and its stature, no less than five feet by summer's end. Its rival for height and beauty is *S. guaranitica* (Zone 7 to 10), covered with indigo-blue flowers.

Salvia elegans (Zone 9 to 10) has pineapple-scented red flowers while the cultivar *Salvia elegans* 'Honey Melon' has salmon-colored honeydew-melon-scented flowers. Clary sage, *Salvia sclarea* (Zone 4 to 9), is the contro-

versial family member. It is loved from afar for its beauty but can be a stinker in close situations (see page 95). It is also a biannual, unlike the other salvias I've mentioned. White *Salvia coccinea* (Zone 9 to 10) is another stinker. It has the odor of a postgame locker room.

Silver clary sage, *Salvia argentea* (Zones 5 to 9), is two feet tall with leaves covered with soft white down and fragrant white pannicles resembling clary sage—but, fortunately, lacking its odor problem.

Syringa sp., lilacs
SHRUB; SUN; ZONES 3 TO 7, ZONE 2 WITH PROTECTION, COOLER SECTIONS OF ZONE 8

Lilacs are probably the best known and certainly one of the most loved shrubs for their famous perfume, sweet yet not overpowering. Strolling through the Brooklyn Botanic Garden's large collection of lilacs when they are laden with blooms is as close to heaven as I've been. You feel as though you are buoyed up and floating in a lake of lilac perfume.

There are twenty-three distinct species of lilacs and over eighteen hundred varieties in many distinct colors, including bicolor. In his definitive work, *Lilacs, The Genus Syringa*, Father John L. Fiala states that none of the other lilacs can equal the pleasing scent of the common lilac, *Syringa vulgaris purpurea* (Zones 3 to 7). The cultivars of the common lilac are often referred to as the French lilacs, not because of their origin, but because of the breeding work done by the French nursery Lemoine; certainly, they are not equally scented. Some new introductions, notable for their larger or double flowers, possess only a faint scent. *S. oblata* has a fragrance similar to *S. vulgaris* but not as penetrating.

While delightfully scented, the Chinese lilacs breathe out yet another perfume, described as an "Oriental" scent—a spicy mix dusted with cinnamon. *S. Sweginzowii* cultivars are also scented, and *S. microphylla*, the little-leaf lilac, is only lightly scented. *S. microphylla* 'Superba' is known as the daphne lilac. Although not a great beauty, it blooms twice, once in June and

again in September. Its only fault is looking a little unkempt at times and a light rather than a strong fragrance.

Father Fiala cautions the reader to beware of the lilacs in the *S. villosa* class (Zones 2 to 7). People find them either odorless or ill-scented, bearing a displeasing musklike smell. He recommends having "both *S. vulgaris* and some of its more fragrant Chinese cousins in the garden to appreciate the differences in lilac fragrances. Each is unique and pleasing in its own way."

Daniel K. Ryniec, the curator of lilacs at the Brooklyn Botanic Garden, recommends three extremely fragrant lilacs: 'Katherine Havemeyer', a pink-flowered cultivar; 'President Lincoln', a blue-flowered cultivar; and *S.* x *hyacinthiflora* 'Excel', a lilac-flowered hybrid. All are singles and descendants of the common lilac, *Syringa vulgaris.*

In gardening there is never only one way to do something. Pruning lilacs is a case in point. A lilac can have the old stems pruned out regularly to make room for the young and vigorous or have the new shoots pruned so it grows into a small tree with from two to five trunks. In season the old-trunk lilacs form umbrellas of bloom. If the gardener chooses the young and vigorous shoots, a full-bodied shrub results with easy-to-pick flowers from top to bottom.

In Saint Petersburg, Russia, an orchard of lilac trees surrounds one of the Winter Palaces. Even out of bloom, the gnarled, craggy trunks have a distinct beauty all their own. They reminded me of a portrait of a hundred-year-old Indian chief in his ceremonial regalia. The strength, discipline, and convictions of his beliefs were all powerfully revealed in his handsome, weathered face. It was the same with the century-old lilacs.

appendix a

Essential Oils and Their Properties

Roy Genders, a British horticulturist and author of *Scented Flora of the World*, classified flower fragrances according to the chemicals that predominate in the plant's essential oil. His classifications help to explain some plant odors and make it easier to describe a scent.

Genders divided the scents of flowers into ten groups and leaf aromas into four. Since essential oils are not pure, some of the placements are necessarily arbitrary. Certain flowers could be equally well placed in a different group. However, an understanding of his classifications is a first step toward making sense out of the bewildering puzzle of scented plants.

FLOWER FRAGRANCE CLASSIFICATIONS

ROSE GROUP An alcohol called geraniol is present in leaves or flowers of this group. This is the delicate old-rose fragrance, the true attar of roses, harvested from damask roses. Not all fragrant roses are listed in this group. Many roses have other perfumes—fruit scents, cloves, or even tea leaves. And conversely, other flowers and foliage, such as scented geraniums, and some peonies, are old-rose scented.

VIOLET GROUP Ionone is the main component in the essential oils of this group. It changes as it ages and takes on the smell of damp woodland moss or freshly cut cucumbers. In its early stage, even insects avoid it. *Violet odorata*, *Iris reticulata* and *Crinum* x *powellii* belong in this group. Orris root, the dried rhizome of *Iris* x *germanica* var. *flo-rentina*, is also violet-scented. It is used as a fixative in the perfume industry to supply violet fragrance.

AROMATIC GROUP In spite of its name, this group is in fact made up of flowers that have a spicy tang, such as almond, vanilla, cinnamon, balsam, or clove. The almond scent is present in heliotrope, *Heliotropium arborescens*. (This is an example of the inexactitude of the science of scent—my nose detects a fragrance more of vanilla than of almond in heliotrope.) Vanilla is a common scent found in witch-hazel (*Hamamelis* species), wisterias, and acacias. Most people agree that carnations, stocks, and pinks are clove-scented. Sweet peas are more controversial, mainly due to the large number and their varying scents: vanilla is only one description, another is a marriage between citrus and rose.

LEMON GROUP Although lemon is found mostly in leaves, there are flowers that also carry this scent, including verbena, the evening primrose *(Oenothera biennis)*, and *Magnolia* x *soulangeana*. Many roses are also included here, since citral, the primary agent in the lemon group, results when geraniol is oxidized.

HEAVY GROUP Flowers with an exceptionally strong scent make up the heavy group. These flowers also contain some indole (the offensive scent in the indoloid group—see below). This explains why some flowers, paperwhites for example, may have a repugnant scent coming as a chaser when smelled up close. Most of these flowers are pollinated by moths and tend to be pale in color: white, pale yellow, cream, or pastel pink. The group also includes lilac, *Lilium candidum*, mock orange *(Philadelphus coronarius)*, some daffodils, honeysuckle, osmanthus, many viburnums, tuberoses, and lily-of-the-valley.

FRUIT-SCENTED GROUP Gathered here are all of the fruit scents except lemon. Roses with fruity overtones (apple, banana, and orange are common rose scents; see the list of rose fragrances on page 151), grape hyacinth, freesias reminiscent of plums, and *Iris graminea* reminiscent of apricot are listed in this group.

HONEY GROUP A light, delicate perfume permeates this group, even though chemically they are closely akin to the animal-scented group. It includes honeysuckle, butterfly bush, scabious, and sweet sultan, *Centaurea moschata*.

INDOLOID GROUP Most of flowers listed as indoloid are from Southeast Asia and South America. Their flowers tend to be brownish and smell of putrefying meat. Fortunately, they are not common as garden plants.

ANIMAL-SCENTED GROUP Often the animal-scented flowers are pleasant enough when they first open. They might have a fruity aroma, sometimes with a musk fragrance mixed in as well. The flowers are chemically similar to those in the fruit group with the addition of a fatty acid. Thus, as Ray Reddell explains it, "a flower in this group may give off a hint of vanilla when fresh but end up smelling like a tomcat." Examples include the crown imperial *(Fritillaria imperialis)* and the flowering currant *(Ribes roseum)*.

AMINOID GROUP Here are the fishy, ammonia-smelling flowers, usually with white or creamy blossoms. Amelanchier, privet, pyracantha, and garlic are examples.

LEAF AROMA GROUPS

Leaves have a wider range of aromas than is implied by their classification into only four groups. They may contain any of the flower scents or leaf aromas. In some cases, the scented geraniums—*Pelargonium denticulatum*, *P. graveolens*, and *P. radula*, for example—have a rose fragrance purer than that of roses.

MINT GROUP This is an obvious category. Everyone is familiar with mint. Many varieties of mints make up this group, even when their scent is mixed with another fruit scent. Scented geraniums and eucalyptus are also included.

CAMPHOR AND EUCALYPTUS GROUP Many of the herbs are included in this group, among them catmint, chamomile, lavender, myrtle, rosemary, sage, and sweet bay. In addition, the Carolina allspice, *Catycanthus floridus*, and the camphor plant, *Balsamita major*, are included here.

SULPHUR GROUP Sulphur compounds are known for their unpleasant smell, often identified as the smell of rotten eggs. In this group are some of my favorite foods— garlic, onions, and watercress.

TURPENTINE GROUP This is the group with the smallest number of members. Its leading member is rosemary, which contains borneol acetate.

Although essential oils can be extracted from many plants by distillation, it is expensive and labor-intensive. The flowers of lily-of-the-valley were used to make perfumes in the eighteenth and nineteenth centuries, but today the cost of handpicking small flowers is prohibitive. It is cheaper and easier to duplicate the scent in the lab.

By analyzing the chemical compound in essential oils, perfumeries and fragrance companies imitate a flower's scent. Chemical equivalents are used in soaps, air fresheners, deodorants, tissues, and all of the household cleaners and cosmetics we take for granted.

A few of the best loved flowers continue to baffle perfumeries by not letting them rob their natural scent. Not only is my favorite, the gardenia, difficult to grow for us northerners but it has refused to part with its essential oils, leaving the perfumery no choice but to simulate its perfume chemically. The fragrance of the sweetbrier rose is another mystery. Its applesauce scent is locked in its foliage, and it too is the despair of perfumery chemists.

appendix b

LISTS OF FRAGRANT PLANTS

These lists are personal, not scientific observations. Fragrances smell different to different people. Some descriptions please everyone; others are controversial. Not all fragrances are purely one scent, some may be combinations of various scents, consequently the same plant may be listed in several places.

floral scents reminiscent of food

ALMOND-SCENTED
Acacia dealbata, mimosa, silver wattle
Heliotropium arborescens, heliotrope
Salix triandia, almond-leaved willow

APPLE-SCENTED
Narcissus 'Mondragon', daffodil
Rosa 'Dr. W. Van Fleet', rose
Rosa 'Gold Medal', rose
Rosa 'New Dawn', rose
Rosa 'Nymphenburg', rose

CHOCOLATE-SCENTED
Cosmos atrosanguineus, chocolate cosmos, black cosmos

Mentha x *piperita cv*, 'Chocolate', chocolate mint
Pelargonium 'Chocolate peppermint', scented geranium

CELERY-SCENTED
Levisticum officinale, lovage

CUCUMBER-SCENTED
Angelica archangelica, angelica or garden angelica
Borago officinalis, borage
Filipendula ulmaria, meadowsweet
Sanguisorba minor, burnet

FRUIT-SCENTED
Allemanda cathartica 'Williamsii', golden trumpet
Chamaemelum nobile, Roman chamomile
Narcissus 'Petrel', daffodil
Rosa 'Abraham Darby', rose
Rosa 'Livin Easy', rose
Rosa 'Max Graf', rose
Rosa 'Medallion', rose
Salvia greiggii, Texas sage, Autumn sage
Tulipa 'Orange Favorite', parrot tulip

LEMON-SCENTED
Aloysia triphylla, lemon verbena
Cymbopogon citratus, lemon grass
Magnolia grandiflora, Southern magnolia
Magnolia virginiana, sweet bay magnolia
Magnolia x *soulangiana*, magnolia
Melissa officinalis, lemon balm
Mirabilis jalapa, four o'clock
Monarda citriodora, lemon bergamot
Ocimum basilicum var. citriodorum, lemon basil
Oenothera biennis, evening primrose
Paeonia lutea, tree peony
Pelargonium 'Prince Rupert,' scented geranium
Rosa 'Parson's Pink China', rose
Rosa 'Pink Peace', Rose

Rumex acetosa, sorrel
Thymus x *citriodorus*, lemon thyme

LICORICE-SCENTED
Carum carvi, caraway
Foeniculum vulgare, fennel
Myrrhis odorata, Sweet Cicely
Perilla frutescens 'Crisps', purple basil
Rosa, 'Sunsprite', rose

MINT-SCENTED
Calamintha grandiflora, calamint
Calamintha nepeta subsp. *nepeta*,
    calamint
Hedeoma pulegioides, American
    pennyroyal
Mentha pulegium, pennyroyal
Nepeta cataria, catnip

HONEY-SCENTED
Asclepias syriaca, common milkweed
Buddleia davidii, butterfly bush
Centranthus ruber, Jupiter's beard;
    red valerian
Chaenomeles japonica, Japanese
    flowering quince
Clethra alnifolia, summersweet
Crambe cordifolia, crambe
Crocus chrysanthus 'Snow Bunting', crocus
Fothergilla gardeni, dwarf fothergilla
Hydrangea quercifolia, oak-leaf hydrangea
Lilium candidum, Madonna lily
Lilium kelloggii, lily
Lobularia maritima, sweet alyssum
Rosa 'Little White Pet', rose
Tilia platyphyllos, bigleaf linden
Tulipa 'Peach Blossom', double
    early tulip

PINEAPPLE-SCENTED
Cytisus battandieri, broom
Salvia elegans, pineapple sage
    (syn. *S. rutilans*)
Rosa 'Buff Beauty', rose

PLUM-SCENTED
Freesia x *hybrida*, freesia
Hyacinthus orientalis, hyacinth

SPICY-SCENTED
Akebia quinata, chocolate vine;
    five-leaf akebia
Cladrastis lutea, yellowwood tree
Clerodendrum trichotomum
    (syn. *C. fragrans*), glorybower
Daphne odora, daphne
Dianthus barbatus, Sweet William
Dianthus caryophyllus, carnation
Dianthus chinensis, China pink
Dianthus plumarius, cottage pinks
Dodecatheon meadia, shooting star
Heliotropium arborescens, heliotrope
Hesperis matronalis, dame's rocket
Jasminum humile, jasmine
Jasminum 'Maid of Orleans', jasmine
Jasminum molle, jasmine
Lycoris squamigera, magic lily
Matthiola incana, ten-week stock
Narcissus 'Actaea', daffodil
Narcissus 'Edna Earl', daffodil
Narcissus 'Honolulu', daffodil
Ocimum sanctum, sacred basil
Rhododendron 'Pink and Sweet',
    rhododendron
Rosa 'Angel Face', rose
Rosa 'Brandy', rose
Rosa 'Crimson Glory', rose
Rosa 'Double Delight', rose
Rosa 'Etoile de Hollande', rose
Rosa 'Frau Dagmar Hastrup', rose
Rosa 'Hansa', rose
Rosa 'Little Darling', rose
Syringa patula 'Miss Kim', lilac
Viburnum carlesii, viburnum

STRAWBERRY-SCENTED
Calycanthus floridus, Carolina allspice
Saponaria officinalis 'Rubra Plena', soapwort

VANILLA-SCENTED

Akebia quinata, chocolate vine;
    five-leaf akebia
Asclepias incarnata 'Ice Ballet',
    butterfly flower
Clematis montana rubens, clematis
Clematis terniflora, sweet autumn clematis
Clematis vitalba, traveler's joy,
    old's man beard
Eupatorium purpureum, Joe Pye weed
Lupinus arboreus, tree lupine
Narcissus 'Carlton', daffodil
Narcissus 'Gigantic Star', daffodil

BUBBLE GUM—SCENTED

Calycanthus floridus, Carolina allspice
Trachelospermum asiaticum, 'Texas',
    Confederate jasmine

floral scents reminiscent of other flowers

CARNATION-SCENTED

Viburnum carlesii, viburnum

GARDENIA-SCENTED

Bouvardia longiflora 'Stephanie'
Mandevilla laxa, Chilean jasmine
Mitriostigma axillare, African gardenia
Narcissus 'Tahiti', daffodil
Narcissus 'Tête-à-Tête', daffodil
Rosa laevigata, Cherokee rose
Viburnum x *burkwoodii*, burkwood
    viburnum

HONEYSUCKLE-SCENTED

Daphne mezereum, February daphne
Hedychium aurantiacum, hardy ginger
Lilium regale, lily

JASMINE-SCENTED

Angelonia angustifolia, angelonia

Lilium longiflorum, lily
Magnolia grandiflora, magnolia
Nicotiana alata, jasmine tobacco
Plumeria alba, frangipani
Trachelospermum jasminoides, star jasmine

LILAC-SCENTED

Dodecatheon Meadia, shooting-star

LILY-OF-THE-VALLEY—SCENTED

Clethra alnifolia, summersweet
Magnolia grandiflora, magnolia
Mahonia japonica, Oregon grape
Paeonia 'Norma Volz', peony
Rosa nitida, rose
Rosa pimpinellifolia, rose
Skimmia japonica 'Rubella,' skimmia
Smilacina rascemosa, false Solomon's seal

ROSE-SCENTED

Monarda didyma, bergamot rose geranium
Pelargonium 'Altar of Roses', scented
    geranium
Primula 'Mark Viette', double primrose

SWEET CLOVER—SCENTED

Dictamnus albus, gas plant
Viburnum x *burkwoodii*, viburnum

SWEET PEA—SCENTED

Rosa 'Mme. Grégoire Staechilin', rose
Rosa 'Ballerina', rose

VIOLET-SCENTED

Crinum x *powellii*, crinum
Hesperis matronalis, dame's rocket
Iris reticulata, dwarf iris
Iris unguicularis, winter iris
Reseda odorata, mignonette
Rosa banksiae, Lady Bank's rose

Moonlighters

nb: night bloomers
pi: flowers bloom during the day, perfume intensifies at night

Latin name	Common name	Fragrance
Akebia quinata	chocolate vine	pi
Allamand cathartica 'Williamsii'	golden trumpet	pi
Brugsmansia sp.	angel's trumpet	pi
Cestrum nocturnum	night-blooming jasmine	pi
Datura sp.	angel's trumpet	nb
Epiphyllum oxypetalum	night-blooming cereus/ Queen of the night	nb
Gladiolus callianthus	peacock orchid, acidanthera	pi
Herperis matronalis	dame's rocket	pi
Ipomoea alba	moonflower	nb
Linnaea borealis	the twin flower	pi
Lonicera japonica 'Halliana'	Japanese honeysuckle	pi
Matthiola bicornis	night scented stock	pi
Matthiola longipetala	evening stock	pi
Mirabilis jalapa	four o'clock	nb
Narcissus jonquilla	paperwhites	pi
Nicotiana alata	jasmine tobacco	pi
Nicotiana sylvestris	candelubra tobacco plant	pi
Nictocereus serpentinus	night-blooming cereus	nb
Oenothera biennis	evening primrose	nb
Oenothera grummondii	Texas primrose	nb
Petunia integrifolia	petunia	pi
Polianthes tuberosa	tuberose	pi
Solanum jasminoides	potato vine	pi
Zaluzianskya capensis	night phlox	nb

Fragrances and Flavors of Herbs

Latin name	Common name	Fragrance
Acorus calamus	sweet flag	cinnamon
Agastache foeniculum	anise hyssop	licorice/anise
Allium sativum	garlic	garlic
Allium schoenoprasum	chives	onion
Allium tuberosum	garlic/chives	garlic/onion
Aloysia triphylla	lemon verbena	lemon
Anethum graveolens	dill	refreshing, cleansing
Angelica archangelica	angelica	cucumber
Artemisia vulgaris	mugwort	medicinal, pungent/bitter
Artemisia abrotanum	southernwood	bitter
Artemisia absinthium	wormwood	bitter, bracing, pungent
Artemisia annua	sweet Annie	sweetly aromatic
Artemisia dracunculus	French tarragon	tarragon
Asperula odorata	sweet woodruff	hay
Borago officinalis	borage	cucumber
Calamintha grandiflora	calamint	mint
Calamintha nepeta	lesser calamint	mint
Chamaemelum nobile	Roman chamomile	fruity
Chenopodium ambrosioides	epazote	pungent
Coriandrum sativum	coriander, cilantro	pungent
Cymbopogon citratus	lemon grass	lemon
Foeniculum vulgare	fennel	licorice/anise
Galium odoratum	sweet woodruff	hay
Geranium macrorrhizum	bigroot geranium	myrrh
Hyssopus officinalis	hyssop	sage/mint
Laurus nobilis	sweet bay	bay
Lavandula angustifolia	English lavender	lavender
Lepidium sativum	peppergrass	peppery, piquant
Levisticum officinale	lovage	celery
Lippia dulcis	sweet herb	sugar sweet
Lippia graveolens	Mexican oregano	oregano
Melissa officinalis	lemon balm	lemon
Mentha x *piperita* cv.chocolate	chocolate-mint	chocolate peppermint
Mentha x *piperita* 'Citrata'	lavender mint	lavender/mint
Mentha x *piperita*	peppermint	peppermint
Mentha pulegium	English pennyroyal	mint

Latin name	Common name	Fragrance
Mentha requienii	Corsican mint	"crème de menthe" mint
Mentha spicata	spearmint	spearmint
Mentha suaveolens 'Variegata'	pineapple mint	pineapple
Mentha suaveolens	apple mint	applemint
Mentha x *gracilis*	gingermint	gingermint
Monarda citriodora	lemon bergamot	lemon
Monarda didyma	bee balm/oswego tea	mint/citrus
Myrrhis odorata	Sweet Cicely	sugar sweet
Nepeta cataria	catnip	mint
Ocimum basilicum	sweet basil	basil
Ocimum basilicum 'Cinnamon'	cinnamon basil	cinnamon
Ocimum basilicum citriodorum	lemon basil	lemon
Ocimum sanctum	sacred basil	cloves
Origanum x *majorana*	sweet marjoram	sweet pungent
Perilla frutescens crispa	purple perilla	licorice
Perilla frutescens	beefsteak plant	cinnamon
Sanguisorba minor	burnet salad	cucumber
Rosmarinus officinalis	rosemary	rosemary
Rumex acetosa	sorrel	sour lemons
Salvia dorisiana	grapefruit-scented sage	grapefruit
Salvia elegans	pineapple sage	pineapple
Salvia officinalis	common sage	pungent culinary
Salvia officinalis 'Tricolor'	tricolor sage	pungent culinary
Santolina chamaecyparissus	lavender cotton	musky, tangy
Tagetes lucida	sweet mace/sweet scented	sweet tarragon
Tanacetum vulgare	tansy	sharp, medicinal
Thymus herba-barona	caraway-scented thyme	caraway
Thymus serphyllum 'Citriodora'	creeping lemon thyme	lemon
Thymus vulgaris	common thyme	thyme
Thymus x *citriodorus*	lemon thyme	lemon
Thymus majus	nasturtium/Indian cress	peppery

Scented Geraniums *(Pelargonium sp.)*

Name	Scent	Foliage Description
'Apple'	apple	round, pea-green
'Atomic snowflake'	spicy	irregular shaped light-green, yellow edges
'Attar of Roses'	rose	velvety lobed
capitatum	rose	wrinkled, lobed, toothed-edged
'Chocolate mint'	mint	green, brown centers
'Coconut'	coconut	small, forest green
'Fern Leaf'	pine	finely cut
'Fragrans'	nutmeg	small, silver-gray
'Ginger'	ginger	round, medium green
'Prince of Orange'	orange	tiny deep green
'Prince Rupert' variegated	lemon	tufts of cream and white
'Snowflake'	rose	lime velvet, edged in white
'Spring Park'	strawberry-lemon	tiny, glossy
tomentosum	peppermint	large, spreading, woolly

Fragrant Peonies

S: single **D:** double **J:** Japanese **B:** bomb

Cultivar	Type	Color	Bloom Time
'À la Mode'	S	white	early
'America'	S	scarlet	early
'Angel Cheeks'	B	cameo pink	midseason
'Annisquam'	D	soft pinks fades white	midseason
'Burma Ruby'	S	shocking red	early
'Cheddar Elite'	J	white	midseason
'Cheddar Surprise'	J	white/gold	midseason
'Cora Stubbs'	J	pink	midseason
'Dainty Lass'	J	shell pink	early
'Duchesse de Nemours'	D	white	midseason
'Festiva Maxima'	D	white	early
'Festiva Powder Puff'	D	white	midseason
'Festiva Supreme'	D	white	midseason
'Florence Nicholls'	D	white	midseason
'Fluffy'	S	white	early
'Fringed Ivory'	D	white	midseason
'Glory Hallelujah'	D	red-pink blend	late
'Jessie'	D	red	midseason
'Lancaster Imp'	B	white	midseason

Cultivar	Type	Color	Bloom Time
'Marshmallow Button'	D	white	midseason
'Mons. Jules Elie'	D	rose-pink	early
'Moon Over Barrington'	D	cream	midseason
'Nancy Nicholls'	D	pink	midseason
'Peggy'	B	pink	midseason
'Pink Hawaiian Coral'	D	coral	early
'Pink Parasol Surprise'	B	pink	early
'Pink Parfait'	D	pink	late
'Port Royale'	J	wine red	midseason
'Raspberry Sundae'	B	white/raspberry	midseason
'Renato'	D	red	midseason
'Rose Marie'	D	cranberry red	early
'Sarah Bernhardt'	D	light pink	late
'Springfield'	D	pink	midseason
'Tom Eckhardt'	J	rose-red	midseason
'Whopper'	B	pink	midseason

SCENTED ROSES

Rose	Scent	Type of rose	Flower color
'Abraham Darby'	fruity	shrub/English	apricot/yellow
'All That Jazz'	old rose/damask	shrub	coral/salmon blend
'American Beauty'	rose and parsley	hybrid perpetual	red
'Angel Face'	fruity/spicy/anise/cloves	floribunda	lavender/crimson
'Ballerina'	sweet pea	hybrid musk	medium pink
'Bell Amour'	myrrh	shrub	salmon-pink
'Blush Noisette'	tea	noisette	white/light pink
'Brandy'	spicy/anise/cloves	hybrid tea	apricot
'Brass Band'	old rose/damask	floribunda	melon/orange
'Buff Beauty'	pineapple-banana	tea hybrid musk	apricot/yellow
'Chrysler Imperial'	old rose/damask	hybrid tea	crimson
'Color Magic'	tea	hybrid tea	pink/cream
'Constance Spry'	myrrh	shrub/English	pink
'Cornelia'	musk	hybrid musk	pink blend
'Crimson Glory'	spicy/anise	hybrid tea	dark crimson
'Dainty Bess'	spicy/anise/cloves	hybrid tea	light pink
'Double Delight'	spicy/anise/cloves	hybrid tea	red blend
'Dr. W. Van Fleet'	apple	climber	white
'Eglantyne'	old rose	shrub/English	soft pink
'English Garden'	tea	shrub/English	apricot/yellow blend

Rose	Scent	Type of rose	Flower color
'Etoile de Hollande'	spicy/anise/cloves	hybrid tea	crimson
'Evelyn'	peach/apricot	shrub/English	apricot/pink
'Fair Bianca'	myrrh	shrub/English	white
'Fashion'	old rose/damask	floribunda	peach/salmon
'Fragrant Cloud'	tea	hybrid tea	orange-red
'Frau Dagmar Hastrup'	spicy/anise/cloves	rugosa	rose pink
'Garden Party'	nasturtium	hybrid tea	white/pink blend
'Gertrude Jekyll'	old rose/damask	shrub	pink
'Gloire de Dijon'	tea	climbing hybrid tea	blush white
'Gold Medal'	apple	grandiflora	gold
'Golden Celebration'	tea/sauternes/strawberry	shrub/English	golden yellow
'Golden Showers'	tea	climber	bright yellow
'Graham Thomas'	tea	shrub/English	yellow
'Hansa'	spicy/anise/cloves/rose	hybrid rugosa	mauve
'Honorine de Brabant'	raspberry	Bourbon	striped crimson on lilac
'Intrigue'	old rose/damask	floribunda	dark red
'L. D. Braithwaite'	old rose	shrub/English	crimson
'Lilian Austin'	fruity	shrub/English	crimson
'Little Darling'	spicy/anise/cloves	floribunda	yellow/salmon-pink
'Little White Pet'	honey sweet	hybrid musk	white
'Livin' Easy'	fruity	floribunda	apricot/orange blend
'Mary Rose'	old rose/damask	shrub/English	pink
'Max Graf'	fruity	rugosa hybrid	bright pink
'Medallion'	fruity	hybrid tea	apricot blend
'Midas Touch'	musk	hybrid tea	bright yellow
'Mister Lincoln'	old rose/damask	hybrid tea	red
'Mme. Grégoire Staechelin'	sweet pea	climbing	pink
'Mme. Hardy'	old rose/damask	damask	white
'Mme. Isaac Pereire'	raspberry	Bourbon	crimson/purple
'Mt. Hood'	old rose/damask	grandiflora	ivory
'New Dawn'	apple	climber	blush pink
'Nymphenburg'	sweet apples	hybrid musk	salmon-pink/yellow
'Oklahoma'	tea	hybrid tea	darkest red
'Othello'	old rose/damask	shrub/English	mauve
'Parson's Pink China'	lemon	China bush/shrub	rose pink

Rose	Scent	Type of rose	Flower color
'Paul Neyron'	rose and parsley	hybrid perpetual shrub	rose pink
'Penelope'	musk	hybrid musk	lemon yellow
'Petite de Hollande'	sweet	centifolia shrub	rose pink
'Queen Elizabeth'	fern, moss/woods	grandiflora	medium pink
'Regatta'™	raspberry	hybrid tea	mandarin red
Rosa banksiae, banksiae	violets	species	white
Rosa eglanteria	apple-scented foliage	species	pink
Rosa laevigata	gardenia	species climber	white
Rosa mulliganii	ripe bananas	species	white
Rosa pimpinellifolia	lily-of-the-valley	species	creamy marked with pink, yellow, purple
Rosa primula	incense scented	foliage species	pale primrose
Rosa soulieana	ripe bananas	species	white
Rosa wichuraiana	green apples	species	white
'Roseraie de l'Haÿ'	anise/cloves	rugosa	crimson/ purple/magenta
'Royal Highness'	tea	hybrid tea	light pink
'Seagull'	sweet	climbing polyantha	white with gold center
'Secret'	fruity	hybrid tea	pink blend
'Sheer Bliss'	sweet	hybrid tea	white/pink blend
'Sheer Elegance'	musk	hybrid tea	soft pink
'Showbiz'	sweet	floribunda	scarlet/orange shading
'Singin' in the Rain'	musk	floribunda	cinnamon/apricot
'Souvenir de la Malmaison'	spicy/apple	Bourbon	light pink
'Sun Flare'	licorice and vermouth	floribunda	lemon yellow
'Sweet Juliet'	tea	shrub/English	apricot
'The Prince'	old rose/damask	shrub/English	crimson/purple blend
'The Reeve'	old rose/damask	shrub/English	deep pink
'The Squire'	old rose/damask	shrub /English	crimson
'Tiffany'	lemon and rose	hybrid tea	pink blend
'Tropicana'	raspberry	hybrid tea	orange blend
'White Lightnin''	lemony	grandiflora	white
'Wife of Bath'	myrrh	shrub/English	rose/pink
'Zephirine Drouhin'	apple/cloves/rose	Bourbon	medium pink

Salvias

Latin name	Common name	Fragrance
Salvia 'Purple Majesty'	sage	citrus
Salvia azurea grandiflora	prairie sage	fruity
Salvia clevelandii	Cleveland sage citrus	woody/camphor
Salvia coccinea 'Alba'	white tropical sage	locker room
Salvia coccinea 'Lady in Red'	scarlet sage	none
Salvia discolor	Andean silver leaf sage	citrus
Salvia dorisiana	grapefruit-scented sage	grapefruit
Salvia elegans	pineapple sage	pineapple
Salvia elegans 'Honey Melon'	honey melon sage	honeydew melon
Salvia farinacea	blue salvia	none
Salvia fruticosa	Greek sage	lavender-scented
Salvia fulgens	Mexican Cardinal sage	fruity
Salvia greggii	autumn sage/Texas sage	fruity
Salvia guaranitica	anise-scented sage	anise/currant
Salvia leucantha	Mexican bush sage	woodsy, burnt cocoa
Salvia officinalis	common sage	pungent culinary
Salvia officinalis 'Tricolor'	tricolor sage	pungent culinary
Salvia officinalis 'Purpurascens'	purple sage	most pungent culinary
Salvia oppositiflora	Peruvian salmon sage	kerosene
Salvia pantens	gentian sage	marigold
Salvia pratensis	meadow sage	pungent/musky
Salvia sclarea	clary sage	medicinal/rank
Salvia splendens	red salvia scarlet sage	none
Salvia thymoides	thyme-leaved sage	thyme
Salvia uliginosa	Brazilian bog sage	aromatic
Salvia vanhouttii	Van Houtt's Brazilian sage	fruity
Salvia veriticellata 'Purple Rain'	purple salvia	pleasant aromatic

Fragrant Narcissi

'Abba'
'Act'
'Actaea'
'Baby Moon'
'Bell Song'
'Big Gun'
'Bridal Crown'
'Canarybird'
'Carlton'
'Cheerfulness'
'Cragford'
'Edna Earl'
'Erlicheer'
'Falconet'
'Flore Pleno'
'Fragrant Pink'
'Geranium'
'Gigantic Star'
'Hawera'
'Hoopee'
'Honolulu'
'Ice Wings'

'Jenny'
'Lemon Drops'
'Louise de Coligny'
'Mondragon'
Narcissus canaliculatus
Narcissus gracils
Narcissus jonquilla
Narcissus odorus plenus
'Nylon'
'Pencrebar'
'Petrel'
'Pipit'
'Polar Ice'
'Suzy'
'Sweet Charity'
'Sweetness'
'Tête-à-Tête'
'Trevithian'
'Unique'
'White Lion'
'Yellow Cheerfulness'

appendix c

Mail-Order Sources for Fragrant Plants

Mail-Order Nurseries

Heronswood Nursery Ltd.
7530 NE 288th Street
Kingston, WA 98346-9502
360-297-4172
Fax: 360-297-8321

White Flower Farm
P.O. Box 50
Route 63
Litchfield, CT 06759-0050
800-503-9624
www.whiteflowerfarm.com

Logee's Greenhouses
141 North Street
Danielson, CT 06239
860-774-8638
Fax: 203-744-9932

Klehm Nursery
4210 North Duncan Road
Champaign, IL 61822
800-553-3715
Fax: 217-373-8403
E-mail: klehm@soltec.net
www.klehm.com

Song Sparrow Farm
13101 E. Rye Road
Avalon, WI 53505
800-553-3715
Fax: 217-373-8403
E-mail: klehm@soltec.net
www.klehm.com

Prarie Nursery
P.O. Box 306
Westfield, WI 53964
800-476-9453
In Canada: 888-476-7303
Fax: 608-296-2741
E-mail: customerservice@prarienursery.com
www.prarienursery.com

Siskiyou Rare Plant Nursery
2825 Cummings Road
Medford, OR 97501

Smith & Hawken
P.O. Box 6900
Florence, KY 41022-6900
800-776-3336
Fax: 606-727-1166
www.SmithandHawken.com

Wayside Gardens
1 Garden Lane
Hodges, SC 29695-0001
800-845-1124
Fax: 800-817-1124
www.waysidegardens.com

Plant Delights Nursery, Inc.
9241 Sauls Road
Raleigh, NC 27603
919-772-4794
Fax: 919-662-0370
www.plantdel.com

The Great Plant Company
P.O. Box 1041
New Hartford, CT 06057
800-441-9788
Fax: 860-379-8488
www.greatplants.com

Seed Companies

Shepherd's Garden Seeds
30 Irene Street
Torrington, CT 06790-6658
860-482-3638
www.shepherdseeds.com

Thompson and Morgan
P.O. Box 1308
Jackson, NJ 08527-0308
800-274-7333
Fax: 888-466-4769

W. Atlee Burpee Co.
300 Park Avenue
Warminster, PA 18974
800-888-1447
Fax: 800-487-5530
www.burpee.com

Select Seeds
180 Stichney Hill Road
Union, CT 06076-4617
860-684-9310
Fax: 800-653-3304

The Cook's Garden
P.O. Box 535
Londonderry, VT 05148
800-457-9703
Fax: 800-457-9705
www.cooksgarden.com

BULB CATALOGS
John Scheepers, Inc.
23 Tulip Drive
Bantam, CT 06750
860-567-0838
Fax: 860-567-5323
E-mail: catalog@johnscheepers.com
www.johnscheepers.com

Van Engelen Inc.
23 Tulip Drive
Bantam, CT 06750
860-567-8734
Fax: 860-567-5323
www.vanengelen.com

McClure & Zimmerman
108 West Winnebago Street
P.O. Box 368
Friesland, WI 53935-0368
800-883-6998
Fax: 800-374-6120
www.mzbulb.com

Dutch Gardens
P.O. Box 200
Adelphia, NJ 07710-0200
800-818-3861
Fax: 732-780-7720

K. Van Bourgandien & Sons, Inc.
P.O. Box 1000
Babylon, NY 11702-9004
Order: 800-552-9996
Service: 800-552-9916
Fax: 516-669-1228
E-mail: wholesale@dutchbulbs.com

ROSE CATALOGS
Royall River Roses
P.O. Box 370
Yarmouth, ME 04096
800-820-5830
Fax: 207-846-7603

Jackson & Perkins
1 Rose Lane
Medford, OR 97501
800-292-4769
Fax: 800-242-0329
www.jacksonandperkins.com

Pickering Nurseries Inc.
670 Kingston Road
Pickering, Ontario LIV 1A6
905-839-2111
Fax: 905-839-4807

The Antique Rose Emporium
9300 Lueckemeyer Rd.
Brenham, TX 77833
800-441-0002
Fax: 409-836-0928

David Austin Roses® Limited
15393 Highway 64 West
Tyler, TX 75704
800-328-8893
E-mail: US@davidaustinroses.com

MAIL-ORDER
FRAGRANT CUT ROSES
Rayford Reddell
Garden Valley Ranch
498 Pepper Road
Petaluma, CA 94952
707-792-0377
Fax: 707-792-0349
E-mail: ray@gardenvalley.com
www.gardenvalley.com

bibliography

Armitage, Allan M., *Herbaceous Perennial Plants*, Portland, Oregon: Varsity Press/Timber Press, 1989.
> *A chatty, highly readable and comprehensive book about perennials by one of America's most respected experts.*

Armitage, Allan M., *Specialty Cut Flowers*, Portland, Oregon: Varsity Press/Timber Press, 1993.
> *A textbook for cut-flower growers.*

Bonar, Ann, *Gardening for Fragrance*, London: Ward Lock, 1990.

Brown, Deni, *The Herb Society of America Encyclopedia of Herbs and Their Uses*, London: Dorling Kindersley, 1995.

Bryan, John E., *Bulbs*, Volumes I and II, Portland, Oregon: Timber Press, 1989.
> *A comprehensive encyclopedia of bulbs that covers so many cultivars it is hard to find a depth of information about a single species.*

Chevallier, Andrew, *Natural Taste, Herbal Teas*, Surrey, England: Amberwood Publishing, 1994.

Clebsch, Betsy, *A Book of Salvias*, Portland, Oregon: Timber Press, 1997.

Coon, Nelson, *The Complete Book of Violets*, South Brunswick and New York: A. S. Barnes and Company, Cranbury, New Jersey 08512; London: Thomas Yoseloff Ltd. 1977

Dirr, Michael A., *Manual of Woody Landscape Plants*, fourth edition, Champaign, Illinois: Stipes Publishing, 1990.

Ferguson, J. Barry, and Cowan, Tom, *Living with Flowers*, New York: Rizzoli International Publications, 1990.
> *Beautifully illustrated and packed with helpful flower-arranging tips.*

Fiala, John L., *Lilac, The Genus Syringa*, Portland, Oregon: Timber Press, 1988.
> *The definitive book on lilacs; highly recommended for lilac lovers.*

Fisher, John, *The Companion to Roses*, Topsfield, Massachusetts: Salem House Publishers, 1987.

Genders, Roy, *Growing Herbs as Aromatics*, New Canaan, Connecticut: Keats Publishing, 1977.

Genders, Roy, *Scented Flora of the World*, Bury St. Edmunds, Suffolk, England: St. Edmundsbury Press, 1977.
> *A textbook of plant fragrances and the compounds that make up their essential oils.*

Jackson, Judith, *Aromatherapy*, London, England: Dorling Kindersley, 1986.

Jellinek, J. Stephan, "Aroma-Chology: A Status Review," *Perfumer & Flavorist*, Vol. 19, September/October 1994, p. 25.

Laufer, Geraldine Adamich, *Tussie-mussie*, New York: Workman Publishing, 1993.

Lloyd, Christopher, *The Well-Tempered Garden*, London, England: Penguin Books, 1985.
> *Every book by Christopher Lloyd is worth reading.*

Martin, Tovah, *The Essence of Paradise*, Boston: Little, Brown, 1991.
> *A wonderful read and a highly recommended book about fragrant houseplants.*

Miller, N. F., "A Preliminary Study of Rose Fragrance," *The American Rose Journal*, Volume 47, 1962.

Morris, Edwin T., *Fragrance*, Greenwich, Connecticut: E. T. Morris & Co., 1984.

Neal, Bill, *Gardener's Latin*, Chapel Hill, North Carolina: Algonquin Books, 1992.

Price, Shirley, *Aromatherapy Workbook*, London: Thorsons, 1993.

Reddell, Rayford, *Growing Good Roses*, New York: Harper and Row, 1987.

Reddell, Rayford, "Making Sense of Scent," *Horticulture*, May 1990.

Reddell, Rayford, *The Rose Bible*, San Francisco: Chronicle, 1998.

Reddell, Rayford, and Galyean, Robert, *Growing Fragrant Plants*, New York: Harper and Row, 1989.

Rogers, Allan, *Peonies*, Portland, Oregon: Timber Press, 1995.

Ryman, Daniele, *Aromatherapy; The Complete Guide to Plant and Flower Essences for Health and Beauty*, New York: Bantam Books, 1991.

Sedgwick, John, "Good Scents," *Self*, October 1992.

Tisserand, Robert B., *The Art of Aromatherapy*, Rochester, Vermont: Healing Arts Press, 1977.

Valder, Peter, *Wisterias: A Comprehensive Guide*, Portland, Oregon: Timber Press, 1995.
   Not much about scent, but good information about wisteria.

Verey, Rosemary, *The Scented Garden*, New York: Random House, 1981.

Wilder, Louise Beebe. *The Fragrant Path*, New York: Macmillan, 1937.
   This book has been republished many times and is part of America's great gardening heritage.

Winterrowd, Wayne, *Annuals for Connoisseurs*, New York: Macmillan, 1993.
   The best book I've read about annuals by a wonderful and insightful plantsman.

index